Martin Johnson Heade in Florida

Florida A&M University, Tallahassee · Florida Atlantic University, Boca Raton · Florida Gulf Coast University, Ft. Myers

Florida International University, Miami · Florida State University, Tallahassee · University of Central Florida, Orlando

University of Florida, Gainesville · University of North Florida, Jacksonville · University of South Florida, Tampa

University of West Florida, Pensacola

University Press
of Florida

Gainesville · Tallahassee · Tampa
Boca Raton · Pensacola · Orlando
Miami · Jacksonville · Ft. Myers

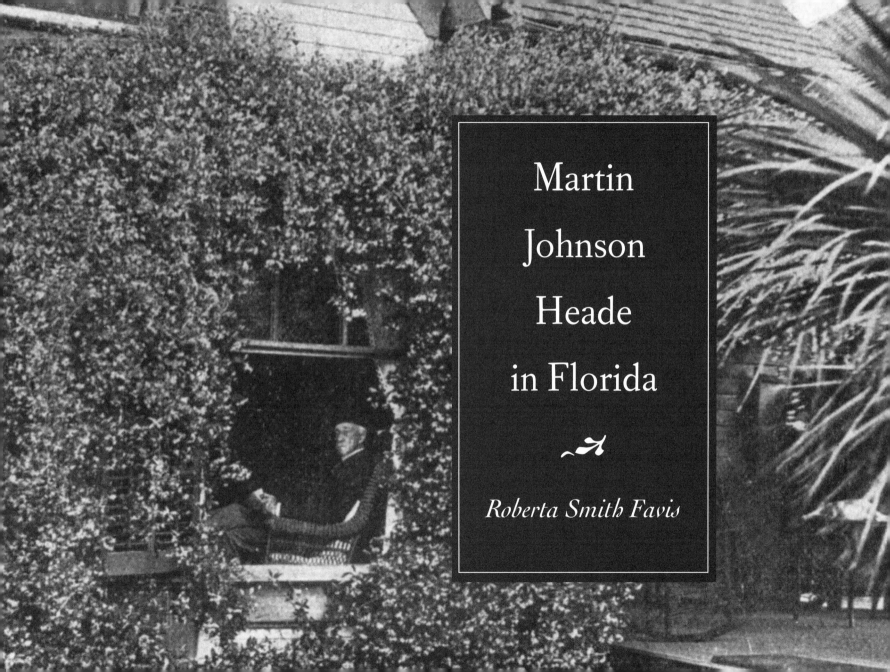

Martin Johnson Heade in Florida

Roberta Smith Favis

Copyright 2003 by Roberta Smith Favis

Printed in the United States of America on acid-free paper

All rights reserved

Publication of this volume was made possible in part by a grant
from the St. Augustine Foundation, Inc.

08 07 06 05 04 03 6 5 4 3 2 1

LIBRARY OF CONGRESS CATALOGING-IN-PUBLICATION DATA

Favis, Roberta Smith, 1946–

Martin Johnson Heade in Florida / Roberta Smith Favis.

p. cm.

Includes bibliographical references and index.

ISBN 0-8130-2661-X (cloth: alk. paper)

1. Heade, Martin Johnson, 1819–1904—Criticism and interpretation.

2. Florida—In art. I. Heade, Martin Johnson, 1819–1904. II. Title.

ND237.H39F38 2003

759.13—dc21 2003042636

The University Press of Florida is the scholarly
publishing agency for the State University System
of Florida, comprising Florida A&M University,
Florida Atlantic University, Florida Gulf Coast
University, Florida International University,
Florida State University, University of Central
Florida, University of Florida, University of
North Florida, University of South Florida, and
University of West Florida.

UNIVERSITY PRESS OF FLORIDA

15 Northwest 15th Street

Gainesville, FL 32611–2079

http://www.upf.com

Contents

Figures

Color Plates: Paintings by Martin Johnson Heade

Color plates follow page 114.

Acknowledgments

I am grateful to colleagues, friends, and family who have nourished my ideas and provided the moral and intellectual support needed to bring this project to fruition. My professors at Bryn Mawr College and the University of Pennsylvania, especially James Snyder and Charles Minott, provided me with the intellectual tool kit necessary for pursuing my career in art history. Joy Kasson and John Kasson of the University of North Carolina, Chapel Hill, and Daniel Peck of Vassar directed three National Endowment for the Humanities Summer Seminars that helped to transform me from a medievalist to an Americanist. The faculty and participants in those seminars shared a rich feast of ideas that has continued to inform my scholarship.

I received a Stetson University Summer Grant to support the initial phase of research on this project and have been assisted in pursuing it by additional travel grants.

The endlessly patient, endlessly helpful library staff at Stetson University, especially the tireless efforts of Susan Connell Derryberry, were invaluable. The staff of the St. Augustine Historical Society, especially Charles Tingeley and Bill Temme, offered numerous helpful suggestions and were always willing to answer my questions about St. Augustine's history and topography. David Nolan generously shared his knowledge about Heade's home and painting sites. Stetson biology professor Terry Farrell answered many questions about bird behavior and the Florida environment. The following also contributed their expertise on issues of Florida history in general and Martin Johnson Heade and St. Augustine in particular: Jeanette Toohey, curator of the Cummer Museum of Art and Gardens, Jacksonville; Sandra Barghini, chief curator, Henry Morrison Flagler Museum, St. Augustine; Timothy Eaton, Eaton Fine Arts, West Palm Beach; Thomas Graham, Flagler College, St. Augustine; and Arthur Marks, University of North Carolina, Chapel Hill. Librarians, curators, and staff at the following institutions also provided helpful assistance: Archives of American Art, Smithsonian Institution, Washington, D.C.; Manuscripts and Archives Collection, Yale University, New Haven, Connecticut; Museum of Fine Arts, Boston, Massachusetts; John Carter Brown Library, Brown University, Providence, Rhode Island; and the Wadsworth Atheneum, Hartford, Connecticut.

My colleagues in the Art Department at Stetson University have taught me a great deal about the practice of artmaking and have provided both intellectual and moral support. My students at Stetson, especially those who have participated in my seminars on American landscape painting, have helped me to refine my ideas. Christine Nelson and Michael McCombs have helped in many ways and provided invaluable editorial assistance.

I owe special thanks to Meredith Morris-Babb, editor in chief of the University of Florida, for her enthusiasm, support, and advice throughout the many stages of this project. Project editor Judy Goffman and the rest of the editorial and design staff of the University of Florida have all provided useful and cheerful assistance.

My mother, Rosemary Smith, my sister, Marianne Mathews, and my husband, Gregory Favis, have all helped with proofreading and also provided incalculable moral support. I am also especially thankful to my children, Jessica, Alexander, and Amanda Favis, with whom I learned to love the environment of Florida.

Finally, this book is dedicated to my grandfather, Dr. Charles Hendee Smith, who opened my eyes to so many aspects of the natural world and first introduced me to a love of art and its history.

Martin Johnson Heade in Florida

Who Will Paint Florida?

THE LIFE AND ARTISTIC CAREER of Martin Johnson Heade (1819–1904) and the early history and images of the state of Florida demonstrate a curious parallelism. Heade's first biographer, Robert G. McIntyre, pointed out that the artist's birth, on August 11, 1819, in Lumberville, Bucks County, Pennsylvania, occurred in a year "notable among historians . . . for the Spanish cession of Florida to this country."[1] During the following six decades, while Heade grew up, became an artist, and pursued a highly nomadic career, the assimilation of Florida into the United States proceeded slowly. The bloody Seminole wars (1835–42) delayed statehood until 1845; then the trauma of Civil War and Reconstruction further impeded development and exploitation of the state. Heade visited Florida in 1883 and decided to move permanently to St. Augustine, beginning the final and most settled period of his long and varied career. When he arrived, the state was still considered the last frontier east of the Mississippi. That would change dramatically as development swept down the eastern coast of the state, ushered in by Henry Morrison Flagler who would also become Heade's first significant patron. Heade was the first nationally prominent artist to become a full-time resident of Florida, and his Florida period constitutes a distinctive and important part of his career.

As we near the one hundredth anniversary of the painter's death (September 4, 1904), it seems an appropriate moment to address the significance of the last two decades of his life and work in St. Augustine. Theodore E. Stebbins, in the catalog of the splendid exhibition of Heade's work shown in Boston, Washington, and Los Angeles at the turn of the millennium, claims that "Heade had the longest career and produced the most varied body of work of any American painter of the nineteenth century."[2] Throughout its run, the exhibition enlisted new admirers for an artist who was never so widely known during his lifetime and who was nearly forgotten altogether in the first half-century after his death. In this current period of renewed interest, as we shall see, the significance of the final Florida works has emerged only gradually. Most recently, the flower paintings that constituted nearly two-thirds of the painter's output during his final years have gained more attention, and the magnolia paintings in particular have been singled out as an original and important group.[3] These flower paintings were appropriate emblems of the territory that was known, from the time of its first claiming and naming by Juan Ponce de León, as the "land of flowers." A dramatic grouping of five magnolia paintings was a highlight of the 1999–2000 exhibition. Disappointingly, only one Florida landscape subject was included in this show, and that painting did not travel to the Los Angeles venue. However, Stebbins's richly revised and expanded monograph and catalog raisonné, which appeared in time to complement the exhibit, demonstrated abundantly that images of the Florida landscape were a plentiful and striking category for Heade.[4] The Florida paintings distilled and refined issues that had been central throughout Heade's career. They are also exceptionally important in the cultural history of the state, because they are among the first paintings to focus the lens of national landscape on this unique territory.

From the time of the earliest European contact, Florida had been invested with an aura of romance and exoticism. The legend that associated its discovery with Ponce de León's quest for the Fountain of Youth suggested that Florida might even be the lost earthly paradise. William Bartram's precociously romantic eighteenth-century descriptions of Florida's crystal streams and fountains and teeming wildlife had even provided an inspiration for the fantastic visions of Xanadu in Samuel Taylor Coleridge's "Kubla Khan." Florida's reputation for flowery vegetation and gushing springs should have made it the ideal embodiment of the New World as paradise, a metaphor abundantly celebrated in the art and literature of the early years of the American republic, but the factors that delayed settlement and development also limited visual and literary representations of the state.

By the last quarter of the century, however, the impediments to both representation and exploitation of Florida were abating. Angela Miller has explored the regionalist agendas that often dictated the selection and marketing of landscape subjects in the nineteenth century. She points out that in the period before the Civil War, "Northern artists had two obvious reasons for avoiding the South—a possible distaste for southern slavery and an undeveloped market for southern views in the North." But she later adds, "In the decades after the war, when the failed search for a comprehensive nationalism gave way to a literary and artistic exploration of the varieties of local experience, the South emerged in a different light, as one region among others. Its past assumed a romantic coloration that denied the ravages of the Reconstruction present."[5]

The scene was set for an artistic and literary exploration of Florida in the postwar decades, but the combination of forces that would enable Martin Johnson Heade to establish an artistic career in Florida was not in place until the 1880s.

Works such as Edward King's *The Great South* (1875), a compilation of illustrated articles that the author had written for *Scribner's Monthly* while traveling through the southern states, laid the ground for a new interest in and attitude toward Florida. King's "enthusiasm for the attractions of the southern landscape answered a new willingness on the part of the North not only to forgive and forget but also to embrace the full potential of reconciliation."[6] The hitherto undeveloped Florida landscape, now pacified, offered tantalizing possibilities for exploitation, and those opportunities are hinted at in the wood engravings that accompany King's text. *Moonlight over Jacksonville, Florida* (fig. 1) typifies the tendency, noted by Joni Kinsey, to present "elevated perspectives, a 'magisterial gaze' or 'prospect' that invited a sense of ownership and conveyed the idea of the availability and potential of the land."[7] The wood engraving *View on the Upper St. Johns River, Florida* (fig. 2) projects a mood of harmony and ease. The calm balance between the repeated horizontals of water and sky and the evenly dispersed verticals of palm trunks anticipates Martin Johnson Heade's compositions of Florida landscape (plate 1). The mood of this image nicely complements the verbal descriptions of the St. Johns River,

Fig. 1. Thomas Moran. *Moonlight over Jacksonville, Florida.* 1875. Wood engraving after J. Wells Champney. Published in Edward King, *The Great South*, 1875, p. 377. Courtesy of Florida State Archives.

for King's rhetoric projects a gentle romanticism onto a type of landscape that had once been demonized as "dismal swamp." "For its whole length of four hundred miles," declared King of the St. Johns, "it affords glimpses of perfect beauty. . . . The very irregularity is delightful, the decay is charming, the solitude is picturesque."[8] These images, published in a national forum, helped to familiarize the country with a new territory and to render Florida both inviting and appealing.

Fig. 2. *(above)* Thomas Moran. *View on the Upper St. Johns River, Florida.* 1875.
Wood engraving after J. Wells Champney. Published in Edward King,
The Great South, 1875, p. 416. Courtesy of Florida State Archives.

Fig. 3. Thomas Moran. *(right) The Road, Fort George Island.* 1877.
Wood engraving. Published in *Scribner's Monthly*, September 1877, p. 656.
Courtesy of Stetson University Library.

The views of Florida that illustrated King's essay, originally drawn by J. Wells Champney, had been transformed into wood engravings by Thomas Moran. Moran was so taken with the verbal and visual imagery of what King called "Our American Italy" that he happily accepted an invitation from *Scribner's Monthly* to travel to Fort George Island near the mouth of the St. Johns River.[9] Here he created illustrations (fig. 3) for Julia E. Dodge's "An Island of the Sea," an article designed to promote the natural beauties and amenities of this sea island near Jacksonville to the "throngs of tourists who every day pass this island in the land of Ponce de León in their search for health or pleasure."[10] Moran's engravings include all of the elements that would become canonical in later Florida pictures for the tourist market: palm trees, sweeping beaches replete with gulls and pelicans, and atmospheric coastal swamps. These widely promulgated popular images were clearly important in advertising the allure of Florida. During and after his 1877 sojourn in the state, Moran also produced a "brief flurry of Florida subjects" in oil paintings, but his Florida views failed to garner the success of his well-known paeans to western wilderness.[11]

Martin Johnson Heade first came to Florida in 1883, only a few years after Moran, but he stayed on to benefit from support and patronage that was not yet available at the time of Moran's short-lived Florida venture. Some of the issues central to Heade's successful painting career in Florida can be elucidated by comparing his view of *The St. Johns River* (plate 1) to the blockbuster-sized *Ponce de León in Florida* (fig. 4), the most ambitious product of Moran's brief flirtation with Florida subject matter. Conveniently, the two works are now displayed in adjacent galleries in the American painting section of the Cummer Museum of Art and Gardens in Jacksonville, Florida. The large and dramatic *Ponce de León* (64¾ in. x 115⅞ in.), the signature painting for the museum since its acquisition in 1996, dominates the first gallery, where it occupies an entire wall.[12] It may take the museum visitor a bit longer to discover Heade's more intimate vision (13 in. x 26 in.) of the Florida landscape, which speaks an altogether more personal and subtle language than the grand oratorical style of the Moran. If we carefully examine the history of these painters, and of these paintings, and the trajectories that eventually brought them to the galleries of the Cummer Museum, their contrasting fates can serve to illuminate the success and significance of Martin Johnson Heade's Florida endeavor.

Moran's large painting was deliberately created to set forth claims for the national status of Florida and, not coincidentally, for Thomas Moran as the painter of that state, in the loftiest national forum, the Capitol of the United States of America. He had hoped to sell it to the Congress, which had previously acquired his *The Grand Canyon of the Yellowstone* for the remarkable sum of $10,000, but he eventually had to abandon his project of placing the work

Fig. 4. Thomas Moran. *Ponce de León in Florida*. 1877–78. Oil on canvas. 64¾ × 115⅞ in. Acquired for the people of Florida by The Frederick H. Schultz Family and NationsBank, Inc. Additional funding provided by the Cummer Council. AP1996.2.1. The Cummer Museum of Art and Gardens, Jacksonville, Florida.

in a prominent national venue. In contrast, Heade's modestly scaled piece was probably sold to a wealthy tourist who would have carried it north as a reminder of the tropical charms of Florida. It made no grandiose public claims but may have served as a subtle lure to entice others to contemplate such a respite from the rigors of the northern winter. Despite his more widespread national reputation, Moran abandoned Florida subject matter rather quickly when he failed to garner the recognition and the commissions he sought. Heade, on the other hand, settled permanently in Florida after a highly peripatetic early career, and there found solid acclaim and steady patronage for the first time in his life. Both timing and temperament played a part in Heade, rather than Moran, eventually becoming the perfect celebrant of the Florida landscape.

Perhaps Moran's instinct that Florida themes would be supported by an alliance of railroaders and other developers, as his western work had been, was simply premature. *Ponce de León in Florida* (fig. 4) eventually found the consummate buyer in Henry Flagler, the man responsible for building the system of railroads and hotels that would open up the entire east coast of Florida. Flagler purchased the painting sometime in or after 1886, probably directly from the Knoedler Gallery in New York, which had acquired it at auction. By this time, Moran had already turned to other interests. Flagler, however, was now in an ideal position to recognize what Congress had failed to see in 1878: that Moran's big

painting was a perfect eastern pendant to the grand western landscapes that had played such a role in promoting western development. Flagler bought the painting for the sumptuous new resort that he was building in St Augustine, a hotel named after the protagonist in Moran's painting. Flagler's Florida resort building and railroad endeavors through the rest of the century would take the lead in opening the flood of traffic that now moves seasonally north or south along Interstate 95. The Hotel Ponce de Leon was the centerpiece of Flagler's vision of transforming St. Augustine into a luxurious destination for wealthy northerners, a "Newport of the South."

Moran's painting seemed custom-made to serve as a talisman for Flagler's endeavor, as is evident if we look closely at its subject and composition. The painting provides a deliberate antidote to the struggles that impeded Florida's early development. This representation of a peaceful meeting with the natives contradicts the historical facts: Encounters between Ponce de León's party and the indigenous Timucuan tribes had been hostile from the outset, and on his second visit to Florida the explorer was fatally wounded. Moran's scene of a nonviolent encounter under spreading trees presents a calculated fiction designed to diffuse lingering unease about the state prompted by the Seminole wars and to replace those associations with more positive ones.[13] He probably modeled his assembly on the archetypal image of harmonious contact between

Europeans and Native Americans, Benjamin West's *William Penn's Treaty with the Indians* (1771–72, Museum of American Art of the Pennsylvania Academy of Fine Arts, Philadelphia).[14]

Moran's composition of the landscape setting has strong affinities with visions of earthly paradise such as Thomas Cole's *The Garden of Eden* (fig. 5), an association that would underscore themes of renewal, regeneration, and healing that rise naturally from the Fountain of Youth story. The conquistador in the right foreground who searches the underbrush appears to be actively engaged in the quest for the magical spring; the shining patch of water picked out by brilliant light in the background clearing may be meant to evoke that fountain. Moran's emphasis on this regenerative theme worked well at two levels: in the national forum of the congressional site in which he had aspired to place it, it would have proclaimed the rehabilitation and also the promise of the Florida wilderness. It would also, not coincidentally, have touted exactly the themes of healing and recuperation that were the mainstay of Florida promotional literature, much of it directed to invalids and consumptives.[15]

It seems that Moran's intuition that a pictorial celebration of the Florida landscape was ripe for exploitation had come too soon, and he had abandoned the field too early. Perhaps if he had persisted he would have found himself, in the late 1880s and '90s, being courted by the new Flagler hotels and railroad lines in Florida as he was

Fig. 5. Thomas Cole. *The Garden of Eden*. 1828. Oil on canvas. 38½ × 52¾ in. Amon Carter Museum, Fort Worth, Texas. 1990.10.

courted by the western lines that provided him with free expeditions to the most picturesque sites on their routes. Conceivably, if he had stuck to the intimate scale (11 in. x 16 in.) and elegiac tone of *Fort George Island* (fig. 6), and been more willing to explore, as Heade would, the gentler nuances and Emersonian mood that Barbara Novak has described as "sublimity through repose," he might have developed a more viable "line" of Florida works.[16] The exploring conquistador in *Ponce de León* seems about to turn his back

Martin Johnson Heade in Florida

Fig. 6. Thomas Moran. *Fort George Island*. 1880. Oil on canvas. 11 × 16 in.
Sam and Robbie Vickers Florida Collection.

on the foreground swamp to seek his magical fountain in the more conventional paradise landscape in the background. Martin Johnson Heade was disposed to examine more closely the moist and mysterious region that this soldier seems about to reject and that Moran would also avoid.

Whereas Moran had struggled unsuccessfully to create a formula that would infuse Florida with the dramatic sense of the sublime he had found in the western mountains, Heade easily found in Florida a landscape completely suited to his talents and tastes, one that many of the painters who specialized in spectacular mountain vistas, precipices, and waterfalls, or even charming pastoral scenes, might have ignored or overlooked. Today we would describe Heade as "a painter of wetlands," though the term was not coined until our own ecologically conscious age. Heade demonstrated an acute sensitivity to the peculiar beauties of this landscape, and his concerns about depredations against the marshland and against its inhabitants figure in a series of letters and articles he wrote for the magazine *Forest and Stream*. These seemingly prophetic concerns have led one recent scholar to dub him "an early voice for Florida conservation," and another to feature one of his Florida scenes on the cover of an environmental history of wetlands in America.[17] We realize now that the swampy lands that developers long sought only to drain and destroy are really the fundament of the biological richness and diversity of Florida. In the twenty-first century it may be more credible to suppose that the true magical spring, or "Fountain of Youth," may be precisely in the murky waters and dank undergrowth that Moran's conquistador disdains, and that Heade chose instead to explore and celebrate. The treatment of the riverine landscape in *The St. Johns River* (plate 1) is characteristic of numerous works Heade completed in Florida.

The distinctive qualities of *The St. Johns River* are scarcely distinguishable in the black and white reproduction that appears among the many closely related Florida paintings in Stebbins's catalog. It shares many almost formulaic aspects with a series of similar works: the strong horizontal orientation created by the 1:2 ratio between height and width; the low line of the horizon, emphasized by numerous parallel elements; the large proportion of the painting given to sky; and details including palm trees, moss-draped oaks, reeds, waterfowl, and the half-submerged branch in the center foreground. Only when viewed firsthand, so that the colors and light are given full play, do the splendidly distinctive qualities of these wetland views emerge. The simple horizontal lines of the composition provide a nearly abstract scaffolding for the delicate array of tints that emanate from the softly throbbing golden glow above the horizon. The tonal play modulates upward in bands of peach, salmon, and lavender, with darker gray-violets marking the upper surfaces of the horizontal clouds. The upper quarter of the sky gradually eases off into muted blue-green, complementing the lower quarter of the canvas where land, water, and vegetation are evoked in more neutral shades of soft sage green and sepia, all infused with an undertone of golden light.

Those familiar with the twentieth-century art historical critique that promoted the reevaluation and reemergence of nineteenth-century American landscape painting will recognize in this painting and this description many of the qualities that have come to be associated with "luminism."[18] Early attempts to define and pro-mote luminism as a category were undeniably of great importance in raising the historical profile of Heade who, along with Massachusetts painter Fitz Hugh Lane, was one of the artists invariably included under its umbrella. Since visual affinities grouped together under the rubric of luminism are not supported by solid historical affiliations among the artists themselves, the tendency to capitalize the term and treat it as if it designated some self-conscious and unified historical group is somewhat suspect. If, however, we avoid overloading the term either culturally or conceptually, it remains useful as a general descriptor.

Matthew Baigell's standard textbook for American art provides a particularly clear and typical characterization of "Luminism" (which he capitalizes and elevates to the status of a movement):

A typical Luminist work shows an eastern coastal scene long since domesticated and settled. The foreground leads easily to an expanse of water and then to a relatively low horizon line. Although internal framing devices are generally absent, precise atmospheric effects and horizontal banding indicate measured recessions into space.... There is minimal overlapping or superimposition of forms. Directional movements within a painting do not often link the various parts and shapes into a tight compositional entity. As a result, forms might appear isolated from each other structurally, but are tied coloristically because of the golden glow or blue tonality that might play over them. Brush strokes and the marks of the artist's individual temperament are hidden and repressed.[19]

Although the first line of Baigell's description, with its reference to eastern scenes "long since domesticated and settled," does not really fit the historic truth of Florida when Heade created this image, the painting itself may be intended to promote just such an image. During the years after the Civil War, when transportation was undeveloped and most of Central Florida was considered too swampy for agriculture, cattle production was the main economic use of the lands along the St. Johns River that Heade depicts. The cows, then, provide the same implicit reference to human use provided by the haymaking activities referenced in the view of *Haystacks on the Newburyport Marshes* (fig. 7) used as an illustration by Baigell.

The details in *The St. Johns River* (plate 1) are so thoroughly harmonized by the soft veil of light and atmosphere that we might at first think that Heade is leaving behind the precise and scientific observation of natural phenomena that he seems to have learned from Frederic E. Church, an artist with whom he had a firm and long-standing historical association. But, just as in nature, as our eyes adjust to the softened focus of his dusky view, we find that he has attended carefully to the precise species of flora: water-lily leaves dot the water in the foreground, bands of iridescent reeds and sawgrass subdivide the water surface, and tall Sabal palms and moss-hung water oaks are skirted by palmetto scrub and vine-draped underbrush. The fauna are also carefully observed, with the three wading cattle providing the only note of domesticity. A flock of wild ducks in the foreground reminds us of what first drew Heade to this area and nurtured his life-long feeling for such marshy places, for the artist was a devoted hunter and fisherman. Thus, it is not surprising that his viewpoint is just above the surface of the water, precisely the position of a sportsman in a small boat (see fig. 17, p. 29). His patient and leisurely attention to every detail of his surroundings, his precise observation of the postures of the eight mallards who are in various stages of swimming or taking off from the surface of the water, and his finely tuned sense of details of time and weather are all quite natural to the angler or duck-hunter. His experience would also have made him aware of hidden possibilities suggested by the lily pads and blossoms that spread across the foreground plane. Harriet Beecher Stowe recounted, in *Palmetto Leaves*, that such vegetation was an inviting signal for fishermen: "The shores . . . now begin to be lined . . . with tracts of a water-lily which the natives call bonnets. The blossom is like that of our pond-lily; but the leaves are very broad and beautiful as they float like green islands on the blue waters. . . . Along the edges of these water-lily patches are the favorite haunts of the fish, who delight to find shelter among the green leaves."[20]

Mrs. Stowe's book provides one of the most vivid pictures of life along the St. Johns after the Civil War, and her home at Mandarin became a sort of pilgrimage station for northerners traveling down the river. Heade made the stop shortly after he first arrived in the state and found Mrs. Stowe "in a delightful mood."[21] She describes not only the flora and fauna of the area but also the ways the land was being developed. She notes the importance of the river grasses as valuable pasturage: "[T]he flats and shallows along by the shore are covered with a broad-leaved water-grass, very tender and nutritious, of which cattle are very fond. It is a curious sight to see whole herds of cows browsing in the water, as one may do every day along the course of this river."[22]

The horizontal position of the twisted dead branch that protrudes from the water in the middle foreground of Heade's painting (plate 1) would precisely parallel the position of the hypothetical boat in which we must imagine the painter seated, and, of course, it represents the position of the viewer of the painting as well. For a boatman, this sort of protruding branch is a dangerous obstacle, a "snag," that signals the presence of some much larger underwater obstacle. This detail reappears in many of Heade's Florida paintings, and one might be tempted to identify it with the dead tree used as a signature motif by the acknowledged founder of the American national school of landscape painting, Thomas Cole. The blasted tree was so characteristic of Cole, who used it as a stand-in for human presence and a reminder of transience, that his followers often included it as a deliberate tribute to the master.[23] In Heade's case, however, it might be better to see this potentially

Martin Johnson Heade in Florida

treacherous branch as simply a signifier of the artist's dual role as sportsman and painter. From the boat, the steersman would need to watch the surface of the water for such possible impediments to navigation, just as the huntsman would carefully observe the habits of the wildlife. It is this practice of careful and sustained observation, of unhurried attention to nuance and detail that gives Heade's painting its particular resonance. The horizontal branch is the threshold across which the artist invites us to pass imaginatively in order to join him in attentive contemplation of this place. For Heade the artist, the dead branch plays other roles; it recapitulates the horizontal theme that is affirmed by the format and restated again and again in the lines of the composition. Its projecting twigs and looping curves rhyme with the trees and foliage in the distance, gently knitting together foreground, middle ground, and background.

Despite the radical differences in scale, style, conception, and ambition, Thomas Moran's *Ponce de León* (see fig. 4) and Heade's *The St. Johns River* (plate 1) do share a great deal. They are both very much part of an ongoing project in which landscape painting plays an important role in expressing and extending the ideal of American nationalism. Moran had hoped to repeat his success with

Fig. 7. Martin Johnson Heade. *Haystacks on the Newburyport Marshes.* 1862. Oil on canvas. 25¹/₁₆ × 50 in. The Walters Art Museum, Baltimore.

western images by prominently assimilating Florida into the national iconography in a major public forum, the Capitol. Heade made no such extravagant claims, but the dissemination of this and similar images through the mechanism of tourism was perhaps even more important in naturalizing and familiarizing this relatively new part of the nation.

The specific physical locales that inspired the two paintings were probably geographically quite close to one another. In Moran's day the original landing site of Ponce de León's party was thought to be near St. Augustine, although modern researchers believe that it was farther south on the coast.[24] Thurman Wilkins noted, however, that Moran's forest glade appears to be farther north rather than south, "presumably nearer the broad St. Johns than the site of the future St. Augustine."[25] The glimpse of palm-flanked water framed by the central arch of trees, if extracted and reversed, would be nearly identical to the vista shown in Moran's *Florida Landscape, St. Johns River* (fig. 8). It is not surprising that both Moran and Heade first encountered Florida around Jacksonville, which was accessible by steamers from the northeast, then pursued their early travels along the St. Johns via riverboat (fig. 9). Available transportation at the time meant that this was a fairly typical itinerary, since

Fig. 8. Thomas Moran. *Florida Landscape, St. Johns River.* 1877. Oil on canvas. 21 × 17 in. Museum of Fine Arts, St. Petersburg, Florida. Museum purchase.

Martin Johnson Heade in Florida

Fig. 9. Unknown artist. *St. Johns River Steamers*. 1882. Wood engraving. From *Into Tropical Florida, or A Round Trip upon the St. Johns River*, issued by the passenger department, DeBary-Baya Merchants' Line, Jacksonville, Florida. Courtesy of Stetson University Library.

Jacksonville was "headquarters of a fleet of steamboats of all sorts, shapes and sizes, plying up the St. Johns."[26] The St. Johns River and its environs also received the lion's share of attention from guidebooks and promotional literature pertaining to the eastern part of Florida (fig. 10).

The elements employed as instantly recognizable signifiers of the Florida setting are also similar in Moran's and Heade's works. Palm trees and water were (and still are) two of the most familiar iconographic emblems of Florida. It is not coincidental that these components are also included in Thomas Cole's *The Garden of Eden* (see fig. 5), because they are also standard markers of the garden of paradise. The Fountain of Youth myth traces the source waters of that mystical spring to the rivers that flow from paradise, and the palm tree is an inevitable part of images of Eden from earliest Christian times. The palm tree even came to be identified as the Tree of Life, the tree described in Genesis as standing alongside the Tree of Knowledge.[27] The earliest booster literature that

Fig. 10. Unknown artist. *On the St. Johns*. 1875. Wood engraving. From Sidney Lanier, *Florida: Its Scenery, Climate, and History*, p. 123. Courtesy of Stetson University Library.

sought to lure visitors to Florida described the state as "The Eden of the South." Of course the idea of America as an earthly paradise had been long entrenched in the ideals of American exceptionalism and manifest destiny, but Florida was one of the few regions that could regularly provide authentic palm trees.

If Moran's presentation of the peaceful meeting of Indians and conquistadors was meant to advertise the venerable history of Florida at the same time it reassured potential visitors that they need not fear present hostilities, Heade's painting can be seen to indulge in a more understated form of boosterism. He shows us the riverscape of the St. Johns as a site where recreation (hunting and fishing) and agriculture (cattle-rearing) coexist peacefully and intrude but lightly on the sweeping harmony of sky and water. In *Palmetto Leaves,* a book that has been described as "the first unsolicited promotion writing to interest the northern tourist in Florida," Harriet Beecher Stowe had dwelt lovingly on many of the details to be seen along the St. Johns in terms remarkably similar to Heade's.[28] As we shall see, Heade's quiet invitations to tropical paradise would be enlisted on behalf of the most aggressive Florida development enterprise of the late nineteenth century.

CHAPTER ONE

Martin Johnson Heade and the National Landscape

M ARTIN JOHNSON HEADE'S contemporaries would be astonished to find that his paintings are highly regarded and much studied in the late twentieth century."[1] This is the conclusion reached by Theodore E. Stebbins, compiling an overview of the history of commentary on the artist for the 1999–2000 exhibition. Indeed, a review of the critical observations regularly published during Martin Johnson Heade's lifetime shows a generally favorable but always rather muted response to his work.

The tide of taste was turning against the group of painters soon to be known disparagingly as the Hudson River School just when Heade was beginning to be identified with that trend. That tide had shifted decisively by the time he moved to Florida in 1883. In Florida, however, Heade continued to receive unstinting (if unsophisticated and uncritical) encomiums from the St. Augustine newspapers. The locals regarded him as their most famous national artist just at the time that his work was being gradually disregarded

and forgotten in the Northeast. The number of works sent out of state for sale and exhibition diminished as he developed a reliable clientele in Florida, and by his death in 1904 he seems to have been nearly forgotten outside of the state. Mentions of his name in general histories of American painting dwindled, and after Samuel Isham's 1905 *History of American Painting* they completely disappeared until the middle of the twentieth century.[2]

The twentieth-century rediscovery of Heade began dramatically with the display of *Thunder Storm on Narragansett Bay* (fig. 11) in the 1943 Museum of Modern Art (MOMA) exhibition "Romantic Painting in America." By this time the curators of the exhibition were unable to give either the correct title for the painting (which had recently been unearthed in an antique shop in Larchmont, New York) or a complete and accurate biography of the artist.[3] The six-line catalog entry acknowledged only that Heade had been "Active 1847–1884." That notation had him disappearing from the radar of the art world shortly after moving to Florida. The timing, context, and the particular picture with which Heade reappeared on the radar screen were of enormous importance in shaping the critical picture of Martin Johnson Heade that dominated the last part of the twentieth century. That his Florida years had been completely forgotten in 1943 was also portentous; the Florida period would continue to be ignored or more or less marginalized through much of the remainder of the century.

Thunder Storm on Narragansett Bay created a sensation at the MOMA show, and soon those who had been heard murmuring "Martin Johnson Who?" at the exhibition were scouring auctions and antique shops and driving up the prices of this hitherto nearly unknown artist. The inky lowering sky and the eerie atmosphere of the painting clearly struck a sympathetic chord for the American audience caught up in the darkest years of World War II, and the haunted mood of the painting would continue to resonate in the bomb-shadowed decades that followed. Robert G. McIntyre was so impressed by the picture that he went on to research and compose the first biography of the artist, filling in some of the gaps left by the exhibition curators. His account of his reaction to *Thunder Storm on Narragansett Bay* is worth quoting, because it establishes the key in which Heade's art and life would be subsequently considered: "I was struck with the force of the thing, with the powerful drama being enacted—a sort of cosmic catastrophe, fraught with a breath-taking sense of elemental fury; or it might be a concluding phase of human existence, the prelude of a new chapter. For a brief moment I felt myself back in the time of the Book of Genesis, though there was no particular literary derivation or allusion. It was like a drama enacted within the artist himself, and projected upon a screen."[4]

McIntyre's perception of the painting as "like a drama enacted within the artist himself" typified a general tendency for the twentieth-century audience to respond to qualities in the work that were perceived as uncanny and deeply psychological. The ground for such responses lay in the popularity of surrealism, which made it easy for viewers in the mid-twentieth century to identify Heade's strange lighting and hyper-real attention to detail with artists such as Salvador Dali or Yves Tanguy. Those perceptions were abetted by the lack of biographical information about Heade, since critics tended to take the scanty facts that were known and fabricate an obsessive and troubled personality to account for the qualities they perceived in the work. Heade's long bachelorhood (he did not marry until age 64), his highly peripatetic early life, his failure to join the usual artists' associations, and the skimpiness of evidence concerning his social connections made it possible, in 1970, to hypothesize a picture of an alienated individual wrestling with his private demons. This view, clearly affected by the critique of abstract expressionism that sees the artist as an existential hero at odds

Fig. 11. Martin Johnson Heade. *Thunder Storm on Narragansett Bay*. 1868. Oil on canvas. 32⅛ × 54¾ in. Amon Carter Museum, Fort Worth, Texas. 1977.17.

with society, does not seem to correspond with the evidence of Heade in his last years in Florida. For many years critics were able to dismiss the impression of cheerful sociability conveyed by the newspaper accounts of Heade presiding over his St. Augustine studio as anomalous, symptomatic of a belated but complete capitulation to domesticity brought on by his marriage. Fortunately, the assiduous researches of Theodore E. Stebbins have substantially fleshed out the picture of the artist's life and personality. His most recent book counteracts the notion of the tortured, angst-ridden loner with a more balanced vision of a sociable and pragmatic individualist. With the help of newly discovered letters, journals, and exhibition records, Stebbins has discovered a new Martin Johnson Heade: "[This] painter was no misunderstood misfit, but rather a successful small-time entrepreneur, albeit one with an idiosyncratic personality. . . . Heade emerges now as a human being, an articulate, sometimes atypical representative of his culture, an American through and through."[5]

With the perspective of this new, more-informed, picture of Heade's early years, his Florida period emerges as a complement rather than a contradiction within his overall career. The following overview of the years before his move to Florida will concentrate on the connections between the works of the last decades and the earlier unfolding of Heade's vocation.

Martin Johnson Heade grew up as part of a family of prosperous farmers in Bucks County, Pennsylvania. His artistic training was skimpy at best, but he did spend a period under the tutelage of the folk artist Edward Hicks (fig. 12). He started by making likenesses in "a primly self-conscious and laboured limner tradition."[6] The first part of his career was spent as an itinerant portrait painter, traveling widely and often to rather remote areas seeking spots where no previous artist would have monopolized commissions for recording the features of the local populace. He also traveled to Europe to hone his skills and to make copies of well-known works to sell at home. During the constant travels that took him to New England, to the Midwest, and even into the Deep South, he also began to dabble in land speculation, buying properties in Chicago in 1853. Alongside his painting, he began a regular series of published writings that ranged from unmemorable sentimental poems to journalistic reports of his travels. Heade was a devotee of field sports throughout his life, and his travels may have been motivated as much by his search for new hunting grounds as for artistic patrons and subjects. From 1880 until his death he regularly submitted letters and articles to the chatty outdoorsmen's periodical *Forest and Stream*.

It has been said of Heade's early years as a portraitist that he "spent 20 years as a bad painter."[7] The period when Heade was growing up and traveling the country in pursuit of portrait commissions corresponds to the triumphant epoch of American landscape painting, yet Heade did not try his hand at the genre until mid-century. By the time he decisively shifted his interest and began to reap admiration and recognition as a landscapist, the apogee of the landscape mode pioneered by Thomas Cole and successfully taken up by Asher B. Durand and Frederic E. Church had already been reached. Heade first began to experiment with landscape in

Fig. 12. Edward Hicks. *Peaceable Kingdom of the Branch.* c. 1826–30. Oil on canvas. 29 × 36 in. Reynolda House, Museum of American Art, Winston-Salem, North Carolina.

mid-century and became a wholehearted convert when he moved into the Tenth Street Studio Building in New York City in 1858, soon abandoning the portraits and occasional genre paintings that had previously sustained him.

In a letter to John Russell Bartlett, Heade spoke with great excitement and anticipation about his decision to rent a studio in the Tenth Street Studio Building: "I feel as if I'd open'd on a sort of new life!" His enthusiastic comments about the studio building, and the clear impact that his tenure there had on the rest of his career, illuminate the motivation behind his shift to landscape painting and also put to rest the twentieth-century notion of Heade as an isolated, tormented individualist. Clearly, his letter to Bartlett indicates that he looked forward to the prospect of close association with other artists and that he was especially enthusiastic about the business opportunities provided by the communal facility. Not only did the building offer "a large and fine exhibition room in which we can show our pictures," but it also promised a steady stream of visitors (and potential buyers) for the artists' levees.[8]

The image that appeared in *Frank Leslie's Illustrated Newspaper* (fig. 13) showing Heade holding court in his studio for a bevy of fashionable and reverent ladies and gentlemen presaged descriptions of the artist as raconteur and entrepreneur that would later be featured in the Florida newspapers. Heade continued to value and seek out similar opportunities for both camaraderie and commerce throughout his career. At different times in his life he occupied quarters in studio buildings modeled on New York's Tenth Street Studio project in Boston and at the Corcoran Building in Washington, D.C. During his Florida years, he became the first tenant of the Ponce de Leon studios in St. Augustine. Much has been made of the fact that Heade never became a member of the many associations and artists' unions that were characteristic of nineteenth-century artistic life, and he himself readily admitted, in a letter to

Fig. 13. Unknown Artist. Martin Johnson Heade's Studio, detail from "Artists' Receptions at the Tenth Street Studios, New York City, 1869." *Frank Leslie's Illustrated Newspaper*, January 29, 1869, p. 296. Museum of the City of New York.

Church, that he was not naturally much of a "joiner." The same letter mentions the exception—he has just become a member of the Union League—as being primarily motivated by the exhibition opportunities provided in its splendid galleries.[9]

Along with general enthusiasm for the milieu and the economic opportunities of the Tenth Street Studio, Heade was particularly excited that one of his neighbors would be Frederic E. Church. In the same letter that described his new studio, he recounted his amazement at Church's *Niagara* (fig. 14): "I look upon it as the most wonderful picture I have ever yet seen."[10] Seeing *Niagara* may have been the single most influential artistic experience of Heade's life. Its basic artistic materials—extended horizontal composition, general proportions of water to sky, meticulous detail, and dazzling light effects—would provide the standard formula for Heade's own land- and seascapes for the rest of his career.

Heade was quick to cultivate Church's acquaintance and advice when he moved into the studios, and he could not resist bragging about his success when he wrote again to Bartlett: "I find him [Church] one of the most affable and agreeable men I have ever met. He is famous for making chocolate as well as in covering canvas. He brings his supply from South America. I'm the *coffee king* of the building & he the chocolate ditto! Tomorrow he's to take coffee with me & then I'm to *retaliate* in chocolate."[11]

The relationship between Heade and Church, who was seven years his junior, seems to have flourished (fig. 15). Heade left his

Martin Johnson Heade in Florida

Fig. 14. Frederic Edwin Church. *Niagara*. 1857. Oil on canvas. 42½ × 90½ in. In the Collection of The Corcoran Gallery of Art, Washington, D.C.

first Tenth Street apartments in 1861 for a five-year interval that would take him to Providence, Boston, Brazil, and London. When he returned to New York in 1866 he moved into Church's studio, and they continued to share the studio space until 1879, Heade apparently acting as agent for Church during his long absences. The friendship with Church endured until the latter's death in 1900 and is documented by a number of surviving letters.[12]

Although Heade was older, he had much to learn from his new friend and mentor. With the exhibition of *Niagara*, Church had clearly established himself as "in a class by himself among the

Fig. 15. *Portrait of Martin Johnson Heade.* 1860. Photograph. Photographs of Artists, Collection I, Archives of American Art, Smithsonian Institution, Washington, D.C.

fraternity of landscape painters."[13] It is instructive to look at what Heade seems to have absorbed from Church, but it is also interesting to note the ways in which he diverged from Church's model. We can get a good idea of Heade's pre-Florida development by examining those connections and divergences under three rubrics: the painting of the national landscape, the artist as explorer, and the artist as scientist and naturalist.

The loosely knit group of landscape painters who came to be known as the Hudson River School flourished from about 1825 to 1875, the second half of the first century of American nationhood.

At a time when Americans were struggling for both a political and cultural definition of that nationhood, landscape painting provided a significant visual tool in the process of self-examination. Martin Johnson Heade's relationship to the artistic discourse of national landscape can perhaps be judged by looking at what he took from Church's landscape, especially *Niagara* (see fig. 14), and also at what he chose to reject or simply ignore. Heade's painting of *Lake George* (fig. 16), 1862, makes a useful comparative example, since it is a relatively rare instance in which Heade chose a subject clearly drawn from the regular pilgrimage route of Hudson River School painting, one that had been recorded frequently by Thomas Cole and his disciples. *Lake George* displays the extended horizontal composition, its exaggerated expanse emphasized by the absence of internal framing devices, which Heade appears to have adopted from *Niagara* and made his standard. Although Heade does insert a thin foreground of rocky shingle, the viewer, as in *Niagara*, seems to hover indeterminately, gazing downward to the surface of the water that nearly fills the space leading toward the equally thin strip of land at the horizon. Both paintings demonstrate a rather dazzling virtuosity in the treatment of the precise texture and transparency of rock and water, but in Heade's painting the rocks are given the most meticulous detail, while the clarity of the water in the foreground rather quickly gives way to an opaque and curiously nonreflective surface. In *Niagara*, the visible rocks serve as obstacles to help emphasize the rush, power, and turbulence of the water whose surface is overwritten with a complex calligraphy of foam, froth, and spray. Church's unusual viewpoint serves to render his well-known subject even more dramatic and sublime, an impression heightened by his careful attention to the theatrical atmospheric effects of passing storm and erupting rainbow.

In Niagara Falls, Church had selected a subject that was "already a veritable national icon that came readymade with complex associations. . . . With its overwhelming tour-de-force of illusionistic realism and its radical composition, *Niagara* recreated the experience of being physically present at the scene."[14] If Church's unusual viewpoint defamiliarizes its subject in order to create an even more spectacular portrayal of the raw powers of American nature, Heade's *Lake George* renders a well-known tourist site nearly unrecognizably mundane. Almost every Hudson River School painter visited Lake George, a narrow, mountain-ringed lake in northeastern New York, and their paintings typically accentuate the specifics of the mountain silhouettes and the islands in order to make the site readily recognizable to viewers. In Heade's painting, the mountains are reduced to a long, purplish ripple along the horizon line, and we are distracted from the clear expanse of water by the humdrum recitation of detail in the flat, rather monotonous shingle in the foreground. Without the assistance of a title, viewers might easily have misidentified the subject of *Lake George*, because

rather than being asked to stand in awe before a spectacular national wonder, they are asked to identify instead with the very ordinary boatman who pulls his craft out onto the untroubled waters. As in the much later *The St. Johns River* (plate 1), the perspective is dictated by the slow, careful scrutiny of the lifelong sportsman. The measured pace of observation is that seen in the second boat, whose slow movement across the middle ground of the composition barely disturbs the glassy surface of the lake.

Church's painting lent itself readily to grandiose national readings, and even the most conscientiously observed naturalistic details seemed to beg also for allegorical interpretation. Tourists to Niagara Falls were regularly urged to watch for the rainbow that could be observed in the mist above the cascading waters. We can read Church's rainbow as a product of scientific observation, but it also recalls the rainbow that God placed above the waters as a sign of his covenant with Noah.[15] In this sense it suggests that such splendid sites as Niagara Falls are also signifiers of a nation specially favored by God. The rendering of the swirling, crashing waters brought to mind the dramatic sounds that were as important to the experience of the waterfall as the visual elements. These effects enabled critics to read Church's picture as an evocation of both the turbulence and strengths of American democracy.[16] As the Civil War loomed, the tumult of the falls and the changeable weather could also conjure the perilous state of the nation and Church's image of the forces of nature could even more specifically be "mustered to glorify the military and industrial power of the North."[17]

Heade's rendering of *Lake George* (see fig. 16) resists such extravagant national associations. Indeed, as noted above, it even resists easy identification of its topographical subject. Heade responds to the quiet immediacies of the natural subject, the ordinary rather than the extraordinary. Throughout his career, with only a few exceptions, he tended to disregard specific sites with recognizable associations, particularly the dramatic verticals of mountains, precipices, and waterfalls that were so prevalent in Church's work.

Despite their different tastes in motifs, Church's growing celebrity must have dazzled Heade, as success followed success in the years following the exhibition of the blockbusting *Niagara*. In the quarter century between his first residency in the Tenth Street Studio in 1858 and his departure to Florida in 1883, Heade would emulate Church in seeking new and unusual subjects, even following in his footsteps in exploring the exotic realms of the South American tropics. Although Church's influence must have been important in Heade's decision to travel to South America, the subjects that he chose to paint there were quite different from those favored by Church. The younger artist even chastised Heade in an 1870 letter for failing to seek out the more spectacular motifs that he himself would have chosen: the Santa Marta Mountains of Colombia. Church declared himself ashamed of his friend for failing to find a good view of the mountains because he stuck too close to the coast, where the foothills obstructed his line of sight. He blames Heade's failure to find the right viewpoint on timidity about venturing into the interior—where he might encounter "tigers and varmints." He promises that he "won't tell Albert Bierstadt—only your good friends."[18] In fact, Heade seemed uninterested in the sort of geological marvels that intrigued Church, and when mountains do appear in his works they are usually kept discreetly in the background, shrouded in mist, with individual features downplayed rather than emphasized.

Church's declaration that he "won't tell Albert Bierstadt" about Heade's failure to pursue the spectacular view of the mountains is revealing. When Heade joined the landscape movement, the primarily eastern subjects that signified the national landscape for the first generation of Hudson River School painters were already giving way to greater and greater geographical diversity. Church himself turned to subjects beyond the national boundaries, though his South American paintings undoubtedly carried more than a little suggestion that the "manifest destiny" of the United States would be to expand its imperialistic reach to encompass the entire hemisphere. Particularly in the years following the Civil War, Albert Bierstadt and Thomas Moran extended the concept of national landscape to the dramatic geography of the West. Angela Miller has succinctly analyzed the ideology of this shift in landscape choices:

Martin Johnson Heade in Florida

Fig. 16. Martin Johnson Heade. *Lake George*. 1862. Oil on canvas. 26 × 49⅜ in. Museum of Fine Arts, Boston. Bequest of Maxim Karolik. 64.430.
© 2002 Museum of Fine Arts, Boston.

"the hyperinflated rhetoric of Church, Bierstadt, and Moran between 1860 and 1875 betrays a need to furnish in paint the sense of conviction that was lacking in substance—belief, that is, in the pre-war ideal of nationhood grounded in a binding covenant between the Almighty and his chosen."[19] Heade, however, seems never to have been tempted by either "hyperinflated rhetoric" or theatrical mountain vistas. He used the "compositional template" of *Niagara* to explore coastal scenes and marshlands, creating moods of hushed contemplation quite different from the bombastic display of the mountain painters.[20]

Northeastern shore and salt marsh were Heade's most usual American subjects in the years bracketing the three South American journeys undertaken between 1864 and 1870. Some of these pictures, particularly those dwelling on the "ominous hush" of impending coastal storms, have prompted suggestions that he may have intended Church-like allegories on the perilous state of the nation before and during the Civil War.[21] Both his associations (including friendships with Harriet Beecher Stowe and Henry Ward Beecher) and his letters confirm that Heade was an abolitionist and a firm supporter of the Union. While in Brazil and then London during the period of the war he waited anxiously for news from home, and he disparaged the British for their support of the Confederacy. Even such portentous-seeming paintings as *Thunder Storm on Narragansett Bay* (see fig. 11), however, can be understood apart from such political meanings, just as they can be detached from the surrealist-inspired speculations of psychoanalysis. The changeable light and weather of the shore were natural subjects for someone like Heade, who loved to hunt and fish. Anyone who spends much time in coastal regions will have observed the almost magical clarity of light that sometimes occurs in the moments before and after the most dramatic thunderstorm. One can well imagine that Church might have made such a subject as *Thunder Storm on Narragansett Bay* into a metaphor for a war-torn nation, emphasizing scudding clouds, crashing waves, and foundering ships, employing a thunderous rhetoric designed to conjure the noisy drama of battlefields. What is striking in Heade's painting is how quiet and still the moment is, how unhurriedly the fishermen move toward shore, reef their sails, and carry their tackle to the beach. We may see the lightning flash in the distance, but we are still counting off the seconds before the thunder resounds and—for the moment—we are captivated by an amazing tranquility conveyed through the poetry of light.

The poetry of coastal light also permeated the marshland scenes that were Heade's most original contribution to the formulary of nineteenth-century landscape themes (figs. 7, p. 13; 18, p. 31; 53, p. 97; plate 2). Theodore E. Stebbins has now cataloged more than 120 views of northeastern salt marsh by Heade, noting that the theme accounts for one-fifth of the painter's oeuvre. It is not at all surprising that Heade should have been the artist to discover this terrain, so devoid of the obvious landmarks preferred by other

Fig. 17. W. Townsend. *Among the Wildfowl*. 1881. Wood engraving. From *Forest and Stream*, January 5, 1893, p. 5. Courtesy of Adirondack Room, Saranac Lake Free Library.

tion, then too the marsh might be seen as an intermediate landscape that lies somewhere between wilderness and the pastoral."[22]

The occasional hunters and fishermen who appear in just a few of Heade's earlier marsh views could be said to be implicit in all of the others. We can be certain, from the artist's own recollections of his boyhood in Pennsylvania, that he first went into the marshes as a sportsman and then stayed on to paint the area he had learned to appreciate through slow, patient observation.[23] The first note that he contributed to *Forest and Stream* pays tribute to the special feeling for the environment developed by the sportsman: "The pleasure of fall shooting does not consist alone in the mere act of killing a bird. The soul of a true sportsman is also keenly alive to the beauties of nature."[24] One of Heade's fellow *Forest and Stream* authors describes the particular joys of "Marsh Shooting" (fig. 17) and the special skills that must be brought to bear:

'Tis true we were after ducks, but the surroundings always add a charm to the pursuit of game, and fortunate is he who can observe and appreciate, even to a limited extent. . . . We have all along moved steadily, no careless crashing through the reeds, no jar of paddle has disturbed the quiet. But now we must exercise the greatest caution, we must steal up to this little pool with the silence of a thought. . . . [No] one may blunder through the marsh and kill game. It is the quick ear, the cautious approach, the thorough "know how" coupled with the perfect accord of brain, eye and finger, that instinctively presses the trigger at the right instant, that has won the prize.[25]

landscape painters. "Why paint the marsh?" asks Stebbins rhetorically of Heade's "quintessential landscape subject": "First, Heade demanded of himself originality, and, though the marsh was familiar and ubiquitous, it was a new subject for the American painter. Equally important, the marsh was simply a place Heade loved: on the one hand it represented untouched nature—an ideal place for hunting and fishing—and on the other it was a natural farmland, where hay was harvested and stacked. If Heade was an intermediary figure between the Hudson River School and the next genera-

Heade was proud of his skills as a marksman, and he brought the same patience, heightened sensual awareness, and hair-trigger responses that enabled him to stalk and surprise his prey to capturing his pictorial subjects. He continued to paint these northeastern marshes when he moved to Florida, at first probably from direct observations made on his annual trips north and, eventually, from memory and imagination. He never exhausted the endless variations made possible by the most subtle shifts of light and color played over a few fundamental compositional elements: winding streams of glassy water, reeds, hayricks, clouds, and sky (fig. 18). In chapter 4, we will return to examine the ways in which these northern marshes prepared his response to the Florida wetlands and also to look at the environmental implications of his prophetic response to this subject. When first recorded, neither the salt marshes of Rhode Island nor the swampy riversides of Florida would have seemed to Heade's contemporaries to possess the dramatic properties called for in a "national landscape." As the twenty-first century begins, the vital role played by such ecosystems in the very survival of the natural world surely calls for a reassessment.

Nancy Frazier has called Heade's salt marsh paintings "mute gospels" and argued that the text for their implicit pictorial sermon comes from the verse of Ecclesiastes 1:2 declaring, "Vanity of vanities; all is vanity." Both the marshes and the type of agriculture they supported were already gravely imperiled when the images were created.[26] In view of this knowledge, the two curious little paintings by Heade, called *Gremlin in the Studio* (fig. 19), can be considered both humorous and poignant.[27] Each work shows a painting within a painting: a canvas depicting a typical salt marsh view is propped on a pair of log sawhorses beneath which cavorts a cartoon "gremlin." The play on levels of reality and illusion seems to anticipate René Magritte's twentieth-century pictures within pictures, particularly when we notice that the water from the painted marsh drips from the lower edge of the canvas and puddles onto the ground beneath. If we mentally extend the artist's conceit, the stream beneath the fictive canvas would eventually spill off the edge of the actual canvas, flowing out at our feet. Recognizing the pictorial joke played in this picture, the Wadsworth Atheneum displays its version beside the *trompe l'oeil* still-life inventions of William Harnett and John Peto. Beyond the joke, however, the painting self-consciously draws attention to the constructed nature of the very art of landscape painting and, by extension, to the inherent vanity of the painter's endeavor. At the same time that the artist reminds us of the frailty of the illusion he has created, he also reminds us of the vulnerability of the landscape itself. The water spilling from the edge of the canvas is also the lifeblood of the salt marsh, the vital element that supports the entire complex web of life nurtured there.

Heade's "discovery" of the distinctive subject of the marshlands

Fig. 18. Martin Johnson Heade. *The Great Swamp*. 1868. Oil on canvas. 14⅞ × 30⅛ in.
Fine Arts Museums of San Francisco.

came quite naturally from his own customary activities. His contacts with artists of the Tenth Street Studio Building, especially Church, also prompted him to join the ranks of "artist-explorers" whose quests for more and more remote subjects were characteristic of the latter half of the century. Barbara Novak's description of the role of artists in the exploration of new and challenging territories remains a classic:

> The landscape artist's prominent role in the exploration of the American continent was as diverse as that great adventure itself. In style, it ran the gamut from the simple topographical description of the early western expeditions to the baroque glorification of the great surveys of the seventies. The locale ranged from desert heat through the climatic extremes of the South American tropics to the icy expanses of the Arctic. The artist was explorer, scientist, educator, frontiersman, and minister. He ran arduous risks and suffered extreme hardships which certified his "heroic" status. The heroism became a kind of tour de force in the vicinity of art.[28]

Heade had always been a wanderer. In his days as a portrait painter his search for new commissions had taken him through the Northeast, the Midwest, and even the Deep South, a territory he found both socially and politically uncomfortable. When he first moved into the Tenth Street Studio, he noted that Church had "an enormous South American scene in hand."[29] Heade must have

Fig. 19. Martin Johnson Heade. *Gremlin in the Studio, II.* c. 1871–75. 9¼ × 13 in. Wadsworth Atheneum, Hartford. The Dorothy Clark Archibald and Thomas L. Archibald Fund.

listened to Church's accounts of his South American adventures in their regular conversations over coffee and chocolate, and he might also have heard corroborating tales from another Tenth Street Studio resident, Louis Mignot, who had accompanied Church on his second South American journey. Church's reports, along with the opportunity to watch the completion and spectacular success of his most grandiose of paintings, *Heart of the Andes* (fig. 20), trium-

Martin Johnson Heade in Florida

phantly exhibited in 1859, must have made a lasting impression on Heade. The "rapturous public reception" of *Heart of the Andes* has been described as "one of the pivotal events of the mid-nineteenth century art world in America."[30]

At the time he was introduced to the prospect of South American themes, Heade was just making the transition from portraiture to landscape painting. He spent almost five years perfecting his landscape skills and exploring the available themes in the northeastern United States and Canada before embarking on his own South American expedition—to Rio de Janeiro, Brazil—in September 1863. This first visit lasted almost eight months, and he returned to the tropics for a brief stay in Nicaragua in 1866. His final South American journey, in 1870, took him to Colombia and Panama. He returned to New York via Jamaica. These exotic travels, an overland journey to San Francisco, and his eventual decision to explore and then settle in barely developed Florida at the end of his life, all suggest that Heade was eager to join the ranks of the "artist-explorers." He may indeed have wanted to identify with the larger-than-life paradigm modeled by Church and described in the passage quoted from Novak, but the picture we get of Heade the adventurer from his letters and his Brazilian journal is, if anything, rather antiheroic. Instead of a mythic champion braving near-impossible obstacles in pursuit of artistic trophies, Heade recalls novelist Ann Tyler's "accidental tourist," someone who seeks to travel without ever having to be uncomfortably aware that he has actually left home. The quests that most preoccupied his writing were for comfortable hotels, palatable dinners, and good society, and he generally grumbled that his new locales failed to come up to the mark.

During his tour of the South in search of portrait commissions, he wrote back to Bartlett that he found Alabama "decidedly the meanest portion of heathendom that ever fell my way."[31] Later he speaks even more damningly of the local residents: "in all my life I never met with such a set of *little soul'd* miserly, every-man-contemptible specimens of the human family as Alabamians."[32] He

Fig. 20. Frederic Edwin Church. *Heart of the Andes.* 1859. Oil on canvas. 66⅛ × 119¼ in. The Metropolitan Museum of Art, New York City.

enjoyed the mild southern climate, however, and recalled it nostalgically five years later from London. As he looked forward to the conclusion of the Civil War he speculated to Bartlett about the advantages that a free South might reap from establishing winter resorts to attract northern tourists. "What a glorious section of the country it would be," he wrote, "and how the people would flock down there in winter if it was leavened with the comforts of northern enterprise."[33] Nearly twenty years later, scouting Florida for a possible new residence, he was most content when he found that vision most completely realized. He discovered that he could now hope to take pleasure in the moderate climate of the South insulated by northern society and northern comforts:

> It seems to me that about every two thirds man I meet is a Northerner. They are crowding the crackers out and devouring their substance!
>
> Jacksonville is like a Northern city, and the hotels—kept by northern men—are equal to any in the North.[34]

The journal Heade kept during the months spent in Brazil in 1863–64 and continued the following year in London regularly cataloged his effort to get into good society. He reported rather smugly on his successes in cultivating the attention of the Emperor of Brazil and members of the nobility in England but was often scathing in his xenophobic commentary on the regular run of the Brazilian and English populace.[35] In the journal and in his letters to Bartlett he indulged in regular name-dropping of the intellectuals and nobility he had managed to meet, but he wrote amusingly and ironically about his efforts to outfit himself suitably for the society he wished to enjoy. To meet the Emperor of Brazil, he "got [himself] white kidded and clerically cravatted" but in England found himself in financial difficulties that made it impossible to buy suitable clothes for a visit to the Duchess of Sutherland.[36]

The social jockeying and quibbling that preoccupied Heade's letters and journal almost make one lose sight of the purpose that took him to the tropics: the goal of finding new pictorial subjects. We are, however, constantly reminded that Heade's social ambitions were closely linked to the need to find buyers and patrons for these new subjects, and in Brazil and England he was especially anxious to secure subscribers and backers for his main project, a lavish portfolio of tropical hummingbirds to be called *The Gems of Brazil* (fig. 21). The content and motivation of these hummingbird studies will be considered in the final portion of this chapter, which examines the artist's scientific interests; however, the subject should also be kept in mind when considering Heade as an artist-explorer. Katherine Manthorne's excellent investigation of North Americans who painted the tropics divides these artists into two categories, explorers and wanderers. Church, she asserts, was the quintessential *explorer*, who systematically undertook scientifically planned surveying expeditions into remote regions. He met and overcame great obstacles to complete his itineraries but regularly returned home from successful missions to transfigure the visual data of his travels into spectacular finished pictures. Louis Mignot, who typifies the *wanderer*, traveled restlessly from subject to subject, and spent most of his career as an expatriate, never settling anywhere for long. Manthorne finds Heade particularly intriguing, because he does not fit clearly into either category. Despite his nomadic life, "he was never driven to abandon his country permanently for the life of an expatriate, and in his later years, he did seem to find contentment." She convincingly argues that all three of his Latin American excursions may have been, at least in part, motivated by his wish to study hummingbirds, giving him a "sense of purpose" comparable to the precisely targeted travels of Church.[37]

Church seemed to glory in the sheer difficulty of his excursions, pushing deep inland into nearly impenetrable jungle and challenging nearly impossible obstacles of climate and altitude in order to peer into volcano craters.[38] Though Heade may have been impressed and even inspired by Church's heroic example, he was evidently not so willing to leave his comforts behind. When the horses ridden by Church and his party gave out from lack of oxygen, the artist dismounted and went on to the top, struggling for each breath in the thin air. The most arduous expedition described in Heade's *Brazil-London Journal* is a two-hour hike up Mount Corcovado near Rio, undertaken too much in the heat of the day so that "by the time the ascent was achieved I had but few dry feathers on me."[39]

The work that primarily occupied Heade during his Brazilian stay was his study of hummingbirds, a project that links the idea of the artist-explorer to that of the artist-scientist. Barbara Novak first explicated the close parallels in the development of the sciences—especially geology, meteorology, and botany—and landscape painting in the first half of the nineteenth century.[40] She finds the apotheosis of this common development, and of a widespread, pre-Darwinian ideal that both science and art are simply ways of revealing and understanding religious truths, in the art and thought of Frederic E. Church. A shared passion for natural science must have been one of the factors that cemented the friendship between Church and Heade. It would, however, be difficult to attribute to Heade the complex scientific/theological world view that has been argued for Church. Heade's science, like his landscape paintings, seems to have been a matter of intense, careful, empirical observation, rather than a product of highly constructed theory. The chief objects of his scientific inquiry were birds and plants, though his exchange of letters with the astronomer Eben Loomis touches on atmospheric observations as well.[41] His many articles for *Forest and Stream* include observations on creatures ranging from rattlesnakes and manatees to raccoons and sea turtles but most frequently discuss the habits of birds.

In the pages of *Forest and Stream*, Heade wrote regularly about his most enduring obsession in the natural world, confessing to having been "almost a monomaniac on hummingbirds" since his boyhood.[42] This childhood fascination continued until the end of his life. A letter to the editor of *Forest and Stream*, penned little

Fig. 21. Martin Johnson Heade. *Hooded Visorbearer*. c. 1864–65. Oil on canvas. 12 × 10 in. Manoogian Collection.

more than a month before Heade's death, declared: "A few years after my first appearance in this breathing world I was attacked by the all-absorbing hummingbird craze, and it has never left me since."[43] Once again, it was a subject requiring attentive and patient observation that captivated Heade, and one that set him apart from his fellow landscape painters, for whom the specifics of flora and fauna were generally only finishing details that reinforced the credentials of paintings as accurate records of the artists' travels and observations. One has to look very closely in a Church landscape to find the identifiable birds or the botanically precise exotics; the occasional sketches he made of such motifs seem to have been intended to add scientifically accurate detail to his vast panoramas and were never primary subjects in their own right. Heade, on the other hand, seems to have gone to South America *specifically* to study his favorite birds. The large landscape paintings that did emerge from the trip were a secondary interest; his primary project was *The Gems of Brazil*, intended to be a group of twenty paintings that would be destined for translation into chromolithographs illustrating an elegant book. As Franklin Kelly notes, it was "the most complex and ambitious project of Martin Johnson Heade's career," and yet, despite the sponsorship of Emperor Dom Pedro II, the numerous advance subscriptions, and a year spent in London trying to get satisfactory prints produced, the book was never completed.[44] A number of reasons have been suggested for the collapse of the project. The chromolithographers apparently failed in the effort to capture the exquisite colors of Heade's originals, and—given the expectations for naturalist-illustrators in the sophisticated audience for which they were destined—perhaps "Heade's *Gems* were too much art and not enough science."[45]

The paintings related to the *Gems* project (see, e.g., fig. 21) are exquisite in ways that capture the iridescent beauty and the mysterious fascination of their subject. Taken with the surviving manuscript of what appears to have been a draft text for Heade's proposed book, along with what can be learned from the letters, the *Brazil-London Journal,* and the numerous hummingbird articles penned for *Forest and Stream,* they give a very complete idea of Heade as an artist-scientist. Heade's research for his project included a careful reading of all the established texts on hummingbirds, the collection of study specimens in the form of feathered skins that he would consult for years to come, and, most distinctively, the careful observation of the habits of his subjects in the field. The primary textual resource was John Gould's *Monograph of the Trochilidae,* a monumental multivolume production with 360 plates. Heade repeatedly cited Gould, and even went to visit him when he was in London. However, he could not resist bragging that, unlike the famous English ornithologist, whose knowledge of this exclusively new-world species was "not made up from personal knowledge of their character and habits, but gathered from travelers and explorers," he himself had studied the birds in their natural habitat in both North and South America.[46] In fact, Heade

also relied heavily on collected specimens for his knowledge of many of the species he depicted, and we have seen that he did not venture into the wilder tropical inlands where some of these varieties lived. Undoubtedly the areas immediately around Rio de Janeiro provided him with ample observation opportunities, however, and he even described having dissected one specimen to try to settle the argument of whether hummingbirds ate insects as well as nectar. (The insects he found in the bird's craw proved that they did.)[47]

The most striking aspect of Heade's hummingbird paintings is the complexity of the landscape settings. By pushing the birds and bits of vegetation close to the picture plane, these paintings reverse the balance of Church's tropical landscapes, where tiny birds and flowers sometimes cannot be detected without the aid of a magnifying glass. Nevertheless, the atmospheric jungles and craggy mountain silhouettes of Heade's backgrounds in these works may be his closest tributes to the younger master. These settings distinguish Heade's images of birds from those of naturalist-illustrators like Gould and John James Audubon who, although they regularly use foliage and flowers to set off their ornithological specimens, include only minimal indications of more distant landscape. As Franklin Kelly notes, "*The Gems of Brazil* convincingly suggest the natural settings in which the tiny birds actually lived, because Heade paid careful attention to depicting the vines, flowers, and trees that made up their principal habitat. He also arranged his compositions so that one looks through a foreground screen of foliage toward distant jungle, hills, and sky, making it clear that these habitats are part of a much greater whole."[48]

The illusion that "the painter has stumbled upon the private world of the hummingbird," and the apparent consistency of the tropical habitat, all contributed to an elaborate fiction.[49] Heade seemed to show the entire life cycle of the hummingbirds—feeding, fighting, courtship, and nests with or without eggs or chicks—although his writings confirm that he was never able to find and observe an actual nest.[50] Heade tried to rectify the errors of artists who had not had his own experience of direct observation, noting, for instance, that male and female birds rarely appear together except during mating season. However, he fell into the common error of amateur naturalists and animal portraitists by tending to anthropomorphize his subjects. The draft of the introduction intended to preface *The Gems of Brazil* includes a long quote from Audubon that extols the affectionate behavior and the "sincerity, fidelity, and courage" of hummingbirds.[51] Writing about his experiments with "taming" hummingbirds in Florida, Heade continually indulged in similar fanciful commentary and even seemed determined to improve the characters of his favorite subjects. Twenty-first-century readers are apt to react with horror to Heade's summary execution of a hummer whose character he failed to reform and to chuckle at his commendation of the "gallantry" demonstrated by an avian "husband."[52]

The utter exoticism of Heade's chosen species, and his sensitivity to the almost magical "otherness" of these little creatures, easily kept his paintings from sliding into the sentimentality that sometimes infected nineteenth-century animal pictures. Recent studies have made interesting suggestions that Heade's hummingbird paintings, particularly the later versions that include spectacular orchids (plates 10, 15), may have been influenced by Darwin.[53] The most lasting impression of his paintings, however, is an effect of poetic strangeness rather than scientific pedantry. The artist himself acknowledged that his representations sought something beyond concrete facts: "For one in the least degree attuned to poetic feeling, [hummingbirds] have a singularly fascinating power which the subtlest mind is unable to explain, but which all who have studied them must acknowledge to have felt."[54] Heade's ability to project the sense of a complete ecosystem whose inhabitants pose and interact in ways informed by direct and particular observation results from an artful blend of imagination and science. He continued throughout his career to create works that combined his memories of South American landscape with his collection of specimen skins and his ongoing studies of hummingbird behavior (most of the latter based on the single eastern North American species, the Ruby-throated Hummingbird).

His best-known and most abundant type of hummingbird image combined the tiny birds with dramatic representations of exotic passion flowers (fig. 22) and, especially, orchids (plates 10, 15).

This combination did not appear in Heade's work until after 1870, by which time he had completed his South American wanderings with trips to Colombia, Nicaragua, and Jamaica that may all have been designed as opportunities for observing and collecting hummers. Heade probably learned the form of the passion flower from books on the poetic language of flowers and studied orchids first-hand in greenhouses where they had become a popular collecting mania.[55] He paired the rainbow colors of the exquisite little birds with the voluptuously strange forms and colors of the orchids, and wove these elements together against a misty tropical background with glimpses of mountains and of vine-draped trees sprouting odd parasitical growths. The twentieth-century rediscoverers of Heade were fascinated by the phantasmagoric qualities of these works and were quick to discern Freudian sexual suggestions.[56] The paintings appear to have been popular sellers in Heade's own day, and he continued to produce a regular supply of them during his last days in Florida. In all probability the buyers were more influenced by the same sort of extravagant taste that inspired incredible ladies' hats of the period to feature entire birds' nests or stuffed hummingbirds rather than by precocious insights into the thinking of Darwin or Freud.

Stebbins's latest catalog includes sixty-six hummingbird and orchid compositions by Heade, with dated examples ranging from 1871 to 1902.[57] Second only to the salt marsh paintings in their abundance in Heade's lifetime output, they show the same willingness as

Fig. 22. Martin Johnson Heade. *Passion Flowers and Hummingbirds.* c. 1870–83. Oil on canvas. 15½ × 21⅝ in. Museum of Fine Arts, Boston. Gift of Maxim Karolik for the M. and M. Karolik Collection of American Paintings 1815–1865. 47.1138. © 2002 Museum of Fine Arts, Boston.

those works to play endless variations on a theme throughout his repertoire. This repetition is partly a demonstration of Heade's pragmatic willingness to continue to produce a supply of subjects of proven marketability. The practice of replaying the same theme also recalls his first master, Edward Hicks, and that artist's seemingly endless variations of *The Peaceable Kingdom* (see fig. 12). Perhaps the juxtaposition of birds and flowers, often from different regions, is also in some way a tribute to Hicks's multispecies visions of utopian harmony but lacking his biblical certainty. The hummingbird/orchid pairings first appeared at a time when Heade had established himself in landscape painting and was adding still-life floral painting to his repertoire. The atypical combined genre shows Heade once again seeking out a distinctive and unusual signature subject, as he had with the salt marshes.

Heade continued to paint both orchids and hummingbirds (plates 10, 15) and salt marshes (fig. 53, p. 97) after he moved to Florida, and the annual visitors to his studio regularly commented on these paintings. Stebbins sees the versions of hummingbirds from the artist's last decades as "infused with warmth and sensuality," and "as much about color and atmosphere as about natural history."[58] The orchids in the final works are derived from sketches that Heade brought with him to Florida (see, e.g., fig. 42, p. 73); the birds were based on the preserved hummingbird skins he had collected long ago in the tropics; and the landscapes were concocted from the time-veiled memories of his youthful voyages in South America. These paintings were the visual equivalents of the stories of earlier adventures with which Heade frequently regaled his studio visitors, born in scientific interest and observation but now thoroughly bathed in poetry and nostalgia.

Heade's Florida finale brings together all of the possibilities that he had, during his early career, enacted in unique ways. Potentially, Florida offered a not-yet-exploited national landscape that deserved to be celebrated in order to memorialize the increased integration of the state into the nation, which took place during the very decades that Heade lived there. Heade kept to his own agenda as an artist-explorer, and though he may have come to Florida as a pioneer of sorts, his willingness to stay on was clearly the result of the comfortable lifestyle, congenial society, and good marketing opportunities that he felt he could rely on there. His scientific interests were most publicly on view in the reports on naturalistic observations he continued to offer to *Forest and Stream*, and—as we shall see in the final chapter—they are also manifest in his prophetic-seeming environmental concerns, concerns no one would then have understood as presaging the as-yet unrecognized science of ecology.

CHAPTER TWO

Searching for the Fountain of Youth

HEADE AND FLAGLER IN ST. AUGUSTINE

W E DO NOT KNOW exactly when Martin Johnson Heade and Henry Morrison Flagler first met, but in 1883 their paths were clearly parallel. There is a romantic similarity in the events that brought each to St. Augustine in 1883, and it is tempting to relate both stories to the mythic figure whose name was chosen for the enterprise that would eventually bring them into closest contact, the Hotel Ponce de Leon. Artist, developer, and conquistador all arrived in Florida after midlife, and each may have been seeking, at least metaphorically, a "Fountain of Youth."

By the time his interests turned to Florida development, Flagler (fig. 23), a founder of the Standard Oil Company, was one of the wealthiest men in the country. In 1878 he had made an overnight stop in St. Augustine during a brief trip to Florida with his invalid first wife, Mary Harkness Flagler. At that time he found the town "depressingly full of consumptives and other invalids." The city made a much better impression when he came back in December 1883 at age fifty-three; this time the city appeared "rejuvenated by an influx of Northern visitors who enjoyed both good health and affluence."[1] His viewpoint was undoubtedly rendered rosier by the fact that he was honeymooning with his second wife, Ida Alice Shourds Flagler, who was nearly twenty years his junior.[2] Two years later he returned and, profoundly impressed by the elaborately staged pageant that celebrated the landing of Juan Ponce de León, he soon launched a scheme to take a more active stance in improving the atmosphere and amenities in St. Augustine. He began plans to build a luxurious resort to be called the Hotel Ponce de Leon (fig. 24). Before long, his projects had expanded to include additional hotels and railroad lines. A gushing article in *Everybody's*

Magazine of 1910 opens with a passage that presents Henry Flagler and Ponce de León as perfect soul mates:

> Fate gave to Ponce de Leon for a ward the daughter of a companion who had died in his arms on the field of battle. . . . She was very beautiful—and very young. . . . After a while his ward consented to be his wife. But he, in his middle age, would be loved as only youth loves and is loved. Once more he sailed over the salt seas, ordered by the king on the old quests and by Eros on a new. The Caribs whom he subdued had often spoken of a magic land where was the Fountain of Perpetual Youth! A delectable vision came to him, and, following its irresistible beckoning, he discovered . . . Florida. . . .
>
> Nearly four centuries later, from the gray North, a man named Flagler, a commercial discoverer, an industrial *conquistador,* past the age of Ponce de Leon, also went to Florida. It may be that he sought the precious gold of sunlight or the turquoise of the sky; perhaps merely a comfortable rocking-chair on a hotel piazza. But he found what his brother-*conquistador* missed. It did not gush from a fountain, but blossomed on the tree of his life's philosophy. . . . He found: his Second Youth. And, like Ponce de Leon, he grasped Immortality.[3]

Flagler and his young bride, like most visitors of the time, began their first visit to the east coast of Florida at Jacksonville. They remained there only a few days and then embarked on the popular steamboat trip up the St. Johns River. At Tocoi, about thirty miles

Fig. 23. *Henry Morrison Flagler.* Undated. Photograph. Courtesy of St. Augustine Historical Society.

upriver, they disembarked and took the short rail spur of the St. Johns River Railroad overland for the fifteen-mile trip to St. Augustine. Flagler found transportation and hotel accommodations in St. Augustine considerably improved, though still limited, and was delighted with the climate. The couple stayed on until March, escaping record-breaking cold in the north, and leaving with the firm intention of wintering there on a more regular basis. When they returned to St. Augustine in 1885, Flagler soon began to develop his plans for transforming the sleepy and rather disheveled town into a tourist mecca, a "Newport of the South."

Martin Johnson Heade was apparently already contemplating a permanent move to Florida when he set off for the state in January of 1883. Heade also began his visit at Jacksonville and then headed up the St. Johns by steamer. He, however, took another popular boat line up the Ocklawaha River toward Ocala, went inland to Waldo, then explored farther south along the St. Johns to Palatka and Enterprise. Finally he turned north again, and then must have taken the same route as Flagler from Tocoi to St. Augustine. He was apparently pleased with what he found there, because by March he had bought a house (fig. 25) and, after a brief trip north, he returned to oversee the remodeling of the structure and to build a studio. The reasons for his enthusiasm for St. Augustine are spelled out in a report he sent to *Forest and Stream*:

> I have wandered, in an unsatisfactory sort of way, nearly all over the State without finding a spot where I cared to stop until I reached St. Augustine, and that I find a fascinating, quaint old place, and is bound to be the winter Newport of this country. The great obstacle in the way of settling up this place rapidly has been the difficulty of getting here and the atrociously kept ho[tels]; but both these difficulties are about to be removed. A new railroad has just been opened direct from Jacksonville,

and the same company that built the splendid house at Magnolia has just purchased twenty acres on the shell road nearly opposite the old fort, and before another season will have a hotel worthy of the beautiful old place, and equal to any in the North; and what is more, there's a fortune in it of no ordinary size. Several efforts have been made to push the city out in that direction, and now that this enterprise is started by a wealthy company property along there will go up with a rush. A great deal has already been bought up with a view to speculation, and when the rush begins next season not a foot will be left, at present prices. Everything now is nicely arranged to make St. Augustine by far the most attractive winter resort in Florida.[4]

The specifics of Heade's glowing report hint that he himself had been caught up in the mood of the developers who were trying to remake the city. If his discourse reads like a promotional brochure, it is not altogether surprising. By the time he penned the article, he was already an active participant in the speculative boom in St. Augustine. The house the artist had purchased was in the middle of the northward push that he described, in the area known as North City (fig. 26). The house stood on the "Shell Road" that ran north from the city gates of old St. Augustine, not far from the most venerable landmark of the town, the seventeenth-century Castillo de San Marcos (also known as Fort Marion at that time). Heade bought the house from General Frederick T. Dent, a

Fig. 24. William Henry Jackson. *The Ponce de Leon Hotel*. c. 1887–1889. Photograph. Detroit Publishing Company Collection. Library of Congress, Washington, D.C.

brother of Mrs. Ulysses S. Grant, and it had evidently been occupied by a series of army officers since its construction in the 1860s.[5] The "pretty little cottage" stood only about a quarter mile from the San Marco Hotel, which was being constructed by Isaac S. Cruft of Boston when Heade acquired the property. In 1889, the road was paved and renamed San Marco Avenue, so that the address of Heade's cottage became 105 San Marco Avenue.[6] The artist's letters to Eben Loomis made clear that he selected the location because he was certain that the new hotel would increase the value of his property and would also bring genial society and potential customers closer to his doorstep. In February 1884, he noted gleefully that his property had already doubled in value and, a month later, he was anxious to buy up an adjacent lot, even though its price had gone up to $5,000. He regularly reported to Loomis on the progress of "the big hotel" and the benefits he expected it to bring to his neighborhood.[7]

Heade's decision to buy a house and settle down, after so many years as a self-described "wanderer on the face of the earth," was prompted by another radical change in the artist's life.[8] In the fall he returned north not only to collect his possessions and painting gear, but also to marry for the first time at age sixty-four. Frederic E. Church wrote to his longtime friend in some amazement: "I'd heard that . . . you had bought a house in St. Augustine and wondered at it. That surprise gives way to the greater one of your engagement."[9] Like Flagler, Heade chose a considerably younger bride. Elizabeth

Fig. 25. *Martin Johnson Heade's Home in St. Augustine.* c. 1890. Photograph. Private collection.

Smith of Southampton, Long Island, was forty when they wed. The artist's old friend, Bishop Thomas March Clark, celebrated the marriage service on October 9, 1883.[10] By the end of the year, the newlyweds were settling into their new home in St. Augustine, and Heade wrote to Loomis: "*Of course* I'm as happy as a possum in a persimmon tree; but we have not yet got things straightened up."[11]

Reports of Heade's life in St. Augustine thoroughly contradict the idea that the artist was either angst-ridden or antisocial. Both he and his wife settled quickly into the social life of the town, and

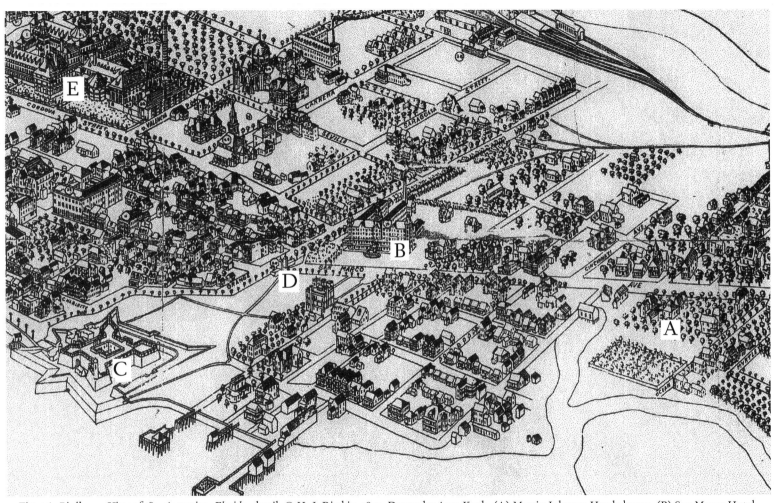

Fig. 26. *Bird's-eye View of St. Augustine, Florida*, detail. © H. J. Ritchie, 1895. Drawn by Aug. Koch. (A) Martin Johnson Heade house, (B) San Marco Hotel, (C) Castillo de San Marcos, (D) Old City Gates, (E) Hotel Ponce de Leon. Courtesy of St. Augustine Historical Society.

their names recur regularly in the *Tatler*, the society paper that chronicled the doings of the resorts. Heade varied a busy schedule of painting and socializing with bird-watching and working in his garden. A steady stream of visitors arrived at the cottage to admire the artist's work or simply to socialize, and friends and family from the North were frequently entertained. Each summer the Heades returned these visits on a trip north. The new Mrs. Heade was clearly a great social asset, and her gracious presence was repeatedly acknowledged, as in this account of "cottage life" in St. Augustine: "Cottage life in this city grows in favor with each returning year, and small wonder with such object lessons as a visit to the Heade cottage in North City will give. Here one is always sure of a welcome from the gracious gentlewoman who reigns with such dignity and kindliness. Here may be found a few choice collections of pictures, the work of different artists and of the master, Martin J. Heade, so fortunate to possess this home and a thousand times more blest that the presiding genius graces his life."[12]

Heade and Flagler may have become acquainted as early as the winter of 1883–84, and clearly the artist was quickly caught up in Flagler's plans when he started to develop ideas for his hotel project in 1885. That year Flagler stayed at the newly opened San Marco Hotel, down the road from Heade's cottage. As soon as Heade heard of Flagler's new resort project, he began plans to build additional cottages on his own land.[13] In June 1885, he wrote to his friend Eben Loomis: "Another big hotel is going up soon, larger and finer than the 'San Marco'—to be called the 'Paunch de Leon'—which means, being interpreted, the internal portion of a famous British animal." As the "monster hotel" began to take shape, Heade issued regular bulletins concerning the armies of men and millions of dollars being deployed on Flagler's projects. When the opening date finally neared, he wrote to his friend: "Why don't you come down and see our big tavern? It's the biggest thing in modern times. It will be open on the 10th of January, and its [*sic*] expected by most sane people that the awful occasion . . . will bring crowds to Florida— may it be so."[14]

Heade continued to mention Flagler regularly in his correspondence and undoubtedly also had early connections with two men who played important roles in Flagler's hotel scheme, Dr. Andrew Anderson and Osborn D. Seavey. Dr. Anderson, a prominent citizen and property owner, encouraged Flagler to embark on the hotel project, sold him the property for the resort, and served as Flagler's St. Augustine agent when Flagler was away.[15] Flagler's relationship with Anderson developed into a lasting friendship; in the late 1890s, Heade was persuaded to return to portraiture, a type of work he had not undertaken for forty years, and to paint a likeness of Anderson for Flagler.[16] Heade may well have had dealings with Anderson when he began to acquire property in St. Augustine, since Anderson was the foremost booster of the town.

Osborn D. Seavey, who was recruited by Flagler to manage the Hotel Ponce de Leon, also played an important role in all of the logistics and planning. Seavey first came to Florida to manage the Magnolia Hotel at Magnolia Springs and, later, the San Marco Hotel in St. Augustine as well. These two hotels were both owned by Isaac S. Cruft and, like most Florida hotels, were open only during the winter months. In the summer Seavey went north to run another Cruft property, the Maplewood Hotel in Bethlehem, New Hampshire. Seavey's brother George was a painter who maintained a studio near the Maplewood in the summer months and who soon joined his brother in St. Augustine for the winters. With Heade, he became one of the first occupants of the art studios built as an annex to the Ponce de Leon. The friendship of Osborn Seavey and Heade is attested by a clipping describing a tour around the state taken by the two men and their wives.[17] Heade and Seavey also shared a common interest in field sports. It seems quite likely that the idea of including studios in the hotel project was suggested to Flagler by Osborn Seavey and Heade.

Henry Flagler was well aware of the important role that art could play in promoting the attractions of his newly developed tourist destinations. The Hotel Ponce de Leon (see fig. 24) was to be a grand Gilded Age extravaganza fitted out with carvings, mosaics, stained glass, and murals. Flagler, who never took enough time off from his business interests to travel abroad himself,

wanted to compress all the opulence and splendor of the European Grand Tour into his resort. In many ways the St. Augustine hotel complex would anticipate the sort of virtual world tourism made available today to a much more socially varied audience at Walt Disney World's Epcot Center.

Two young architects, John M. Carrère and Thomas Hastings, were entrusted with the design of the Ponce de Leon complex. The fame they accrued through working on Flagler projects would lead to many important future commissions, including the New York Public Library.[18] The building they created was a sort of Spanish Renaissance confection, designed to evoke all of the most fanciful and exotic associations its theme might embody. An early tribute emphasized the way in which the architects sought to blend the picturesque historical associations and the appearance of the existing city:

They visioned not merely a conventional big hotel, but a pleasure palace, embodying the characteristics of Spanish Renaissance architecture, with sunny courts and cool retreats, fountains and towers, and decorations suggestive of the history of the city.

Standing within sound of the surf on the Florida shore, its towers overlooking the sea, it should be named in honor of the Discoverer whose romantic quest had made his name typical of the adventurous and chimerical spirit of his age. And as the bastions and watchtowers of the Fort were significant of the military might of sixteenth century

Spain, so this new memorial, in beauty and harmony of parts, shall be a reminder of that other Spain, the mother of artists and architects and cunning craftsmen.[19]

Carrère and Hastings used three elements to harmonize their immense structure with the older buildings of the town: overhanging balconies characteristic of the Spanish style of many old St. Augustine houses, prominent arches, and the coquina stone texture of the walls.[20] If the Hotel Ponce de Leon reminds us a bit of a multi-turreted sand castle, the association may be quite apt. Beneath the elaborate historicizing frosting was a building that employed the latest technology of cast-in-place concrete, made of an amalgam compounded from the local coquina-shell rock quarried at the nearby seashore on Anastasia Island. The cool gray of the coquina-concrete was offset by decorations of salmon-colored terra-cotta tile. The wooden trim of balconies and windows was painted in a distinctive bright tone that would become known as "Flagler yellow," since it would be used in his later hotel projects and even on the passenger cars of his railroad.[21] The seemingly fanciful details often concealed practical functions: a fountain on the grounds served to aerate the sulfur water that was pumped from a deep artesian well; the twin towers housed large water tanks used to maintain water pressure in the hotel. Interior amenities included electric lights and elevators as well as lavish furnishings.[22] The 1887 promotional brochure titled *Florida, the American Riviera; St.*

Fig. 27. *Rotunda of the Ponce de Leon Hotel.* c. 1887–1901. Photograph. © Henry Morrison Flagler Museum Archives, Palm Beach, Florida.

Augustine, the Winter Newport, announced: "We claim that the daydreams of the sixteenth century have become the realizations of the nineteenth, and that the true Elixir of Life is to be found in this incomparable treasury of balmy airs, golden sunshine and health-giving waters. Like the inexhaustible stores of mineral wealth hidden away in the vast recesses of the American continent and upon which the almighty has set his 'timelock' those treasures await only the 'open sesame' of modern progress and effort."[23]

Art of all sorts played an important role in the interior décor. The great rotunda (fig. 27) and dining hall featured elaborate allegorical murals by George W. Maynard. Elegant stained glass windows designed by Louis Comfort Tiffany illuminated the dining room, where more painted allegories covered the ceiling. The grand parlor (fig. 28), divided into more intimate spaces by means of arches, was transformed into a cozy bower by the ceiling paintings of Virgilio Tojetti. "The plump cherubs and doves portrayed in his paintings," notes historian Thomas Graham, "embodied a late-Victorian concept of youthfulness—a fitting theme in the land of the fountain of youth."[24]

A variety of paintings by other artists hung throughout the hotel. In the grand parlor, the series of eight portraits by Joszi Arpád Koppay of Polish actress Helena Modjesha dressed for different Shakespearian roles drew frequent comments. Two large oak-framed history paintings showing *Columbus Discovering America* and *Introduction of Christianity to the Huns* decorated the second floor interior lobby.[25] Early photographs of the interior (figs. 27, 28) show that numerous other framed paintings complemented the rich furnishings of all the public rooms, but they are usually difficult to identify. The subjects visible in the photographs seem most often to be figurative paintings, but Flagler bought flower paintings and landscapes for the hotel as well. Sandra Barghini has recently established an extensive list of paintings once owned by Flagler, including many purchased from Knoedler and Company in New York between 1879 and 1888, and we now have a much more complete idea of Flagler's collecting tastes.[26] Most of

Fig. 28. William Henry Jackson. *Parlor of the Ponce de Leon Hotel.* c. 1887–89. Photograph. Detroit Publishing Company Collection. Library of Congress, Washington, D.C.

Martin Johnson Heade in Florida

the paintings he purchased for his homes and for his hotels were academic in style and historic or romantic in subject, and he seems to have had a particular taste for the sensual Orientalist themes popular at the end of the nineteenth century. Such works would have nicely complemented the exotic pretensions of the décor of the Ponce de Leon, and probably at least some of them were displayed there. Many of the elegantly framed figurative works in the parlors and rotunda were probably purchased in the North along with other lavish accoutrements that were shipped to St. Augustine; but Flagler would also steadily add flower paintings and landscapes by artists working in St. Augustine.

When Flagler bought Moran's *Ponce de León in Florida* (fig. 4, p. 6), he must have planned to feature it prominently in the hotel decoration, although there is no clear evidence of exactly when and where the painting hung in the resort.[27] Certainly the painting was perfectly suited to create a near-trademark image for the complex, but its large size may have made it difficult to fit into spaces that were already cluttered with decorative detail. The most likely locales seem to be the large walls in the parlor or the second story of the rotunda, where two large paintings commissioned from Heade were installed. In 1901, Flagler's interests were increasingly concentrated further south, and he transferred the Moran and the Heade paintings to his new residence (fig. 29), Whitehall, in Palm Beach.[28] Perhaps it was not entirely coincidental that Whitehall had

Fig. 29. *Italian Renaissance Library, Whitehall.* 1903. Photograph. © Henry Morrison Flagler Museum Archives, Palm Beach, Florida.

been built for Flagler's third wife, Mary Lily Kenan Flagler, who was only thirty-four when she wed the seventy-one-year-old Flagler. The suggestive reference to the Fountain of Youth must have seemed more apropos than ever.

In 1886, probably the same year that he acquired the Moran work, Flagler also bought one of the largest paintings in Heade's studio. He followed this major purchase by immediately commissioning Heade to create two even larger works for the upper rotunda of his hotel. The first Heade painting Flagler selected was *The Great Florida Marsh* (plate 4). This impressive piece includes many of the elements already cataloged in the later *The St. Johns River* (plate 1): moss-draped oaks, palms and palmettos, reeds and vine-tangled underbrush, a horizontal snag serving as a roost for water birds, and the water lilies sprinkled across the surface of the relatively still water. A clump of trees and bushes to the left and a variety of plants characteristic of freshwater swamps are pushed close to the foreground plane, so that many can be precisely identified. The trees with bulbous bottoms that grow directly in the water may be swamp tupelo. The large heart-shaped leaves of arum (elephant ear) fill the left corner; white water lilies and the narrower leaved spatterdock (with tight yellow blooms) are interspersed with shaggy clumps of wetland grasses. The varied vegetation and the grazing cattle in the grassy strip of the middle ground are clues that this is probably another view of the St. Johns River, possibly the flat upper reaches above Lake Monroe where the main stream narrows and sometimes nearly disappears in marshy side channels.[29]

Both Flagler and Heade were among the majority of tourists to Florida who would associate their first experience of the region with a picturesque boat ride down the St. Johns. Therefore it seems appropriate for Flagler to have selected a view of the St. Johns as a canonical image of the eastern wilderness that he would play such a central role in opening to development. Moran (fig. 8, p. 14) and several other northern artists who visited Florida before Heade, including John Bristol, William Morris Hunt, George McCord, and Alexander Wyant, had all painted views along the St. Johns.[30] Stebbins claims that the scene depicted in *The Great Florida Marsh* "could be anywhere in the equatorial zones," and is meant to convey "the tropics as a generalized experience, a state of mind," but there are enough specifics in the painting to indicate that Heade meant for viewers to recognize a particular and well-known part of Florida.[31]

The Great Florida Marsh was certainly one of the largest Florida paintings in Heade's studio when Flagler made his selection. Another painting of the same size (about 28 x 54 in.), *Florida Sunrise* (plate 7), also portrays the St. Johns and seems to have been painted at about the same time.[32] The paintings would have made appropriate pendants, since *Florida Sunrise* appears to show the wide, easily navigable open stretches of the river near its delta at Jacksonville, contrasting with the upper St. Johns as shown in *The Great Florida Marsh*. The elaborate masthead for *The St. Augustine News* (fig. 30) depicts a remarkably similar arrangement of palms and palmettos, along with boats that seem shrunken to toylike scale by the wide expanse of water. The parasol-toting putto who perches jauntily on the lower curve of the "S" suggests that here, in

Fig. 30. Masthead, *St. Augustine News*, January 18, 1891.
Courtesy of St. Augustine Historical Society.

the sunshine and natural waterways of Florida, was the real Fountain of Youth. Heade's *Florida Sunrise*, in which the sun's rays burst from the horizon with the force of resurrection, would have conveyed the same message in a less obvious manner.

Interestingly, *Florida Sunrise* was eventually destined for a prominent national forum of the type that had eluded Moran's *Ponce de León in Florida* (fig. 4, p. 6). After passing through various hands, it was purchased at auction by one of Henry Flagler's descendents in 1977 and, in the following year, was presented to the nation for the collection of the White House.[33] Heade clearly felt

that views of the St. Johns would represent Florida appropriately in the forum of national landscape; in his first years in Florida he sent paintings of the St. Johns north to a New York dealer; to the Southern Exposition in Louisville, Kentucky; to the National Academy of Design in New York City; and to his friend Eben Loomis in Washington, D.C., who he hoped would sell the painting for him.[34] The reporter who visited his studio shortly after the opening of the Hotel Ponce de Leon wrote that "a river scene taken on the upper St. Johns, near Enterprise," was "one of the best works in his studio."[35]

Although the boat ride up the St. Johns was gradually being replaced as the standard entrance to the state's east coast by the improved rail system, the river remained important for both commerce and recreation. While building the Ponce de Leon, Flagler was also ensuring that access to St. Augustine would be as easy and comfortable as possible for prospective guests. The luxurious electrically lit vestibule trains that conveyed the first visitors to the hotel when it opened moved along an increasingly seamless network of rail lines. After Flagler constructed steel bridges across the St. Johns, easterners could make a continuous train journey from New York to St. Augustine all on a plush all-Pullman train in only thirty-six hours. However, Flagler also built or improved lines to Tocoi and Palatka as well as Jacksonville, so it remained quite easy for hotel guests to have ready access to the sights of the St. Johns.

At one point Flagler hoped to add a hotel in Palatka to his growing stable of resort properties, but even when he failed to obtain the land he wanted he continued to visit and buy land on other parts of the St. Johns, and to establish endeavors there ranging from orange groves to a model farm.[36] Heade's jaunts to the St. Johns for sketching or for hunting and fishing must also have been assisted by the convenient new rail lines.

Flagler followed his first purchase with a commission for two even larger works to be hung in the Hotel Ponce de Leon, offering the artist $2000 for each. This was the same sum fetched by Thomas Moran's *Ponce de León in Florida* when it was auctioned at Ortgies sale on February 25, 1886, undoubtedly a great disappointment to the artist who had at one time hoped to sell the painting to the nation for $10,000 and to see it hung in a prominent national setting.[37] Although the two works (7½ ft. and 8 ft. wide respectively) that Martin Johnson Heade painted on commission for Henry Flagler's hotel were the largest of his career, they still fell short of the scale of Moran's big painting. Heade, however, was thoroughly delighted with the price paid for each of these works. Considering that, in 1884, he had been desperately urging his friend Eben Loomis to try to sell his St. Johns River view in Washington for $200, the relative inflation of the price tag must have seemed much greater than the mere increase in the size of the canvas. Inch for inch, this was still clearly the highest figure a Heade painting had

fetched thus far, and one can practically hear the glee in his voice as he announced to Loomis: "I'm painting two landscapes for [Flagler] . . . which will take some thousands out of his pocket, but I think he can stand it. Croesus' fortune was about 17,000,000—as nigh as I can come to it—but Flagler wouldn't take 25,000,000 for his'n. Standard ile [*sic*] done it!" We don't know what Flagler paid for the Moran when he bought it from Knoedler's Gallery in the years after the Ortgies sale, but presumably the figure remained comparable to the fees he was paying to Heade. It is no wonder that Heade bragged again to Loomis as his paintings neared completion: "My two big pictures, for the parlor of the hotel are nearly completed. One is a Jamaica picture, with tree ferns and things and I think it's a pretty neat thing—for me. The other is a Florida scene, a sunset. St. Augustine is going to be great fun!"[38] The paintings were installed in the second level of the rotunda (see fig. 27), where *The Great Florida Sunset* can just be discerned in an early photograph.[39]

The Great Florida Sunset appears to show another view of the St. Johns, with a few grazing cattle barely visible on the distant bank. The composition and many of the details are similar to *The Great Florida Marsh* (plate 4), but the overall effect is quite different. The sunset motif allowed Heade to orchestrate a delicious array of complementary rose and green tones; and the larger expanse of reflective water surface enabled him to play an elegant counterpoint to the pearls and pinks of the sky with bright salmons and deep gray-greens. The water surface is enlivened with a scattering of cypress knees and white and yellow lilies, and a number of wading and swimming birds are artfully dispersed at intervals to mark off the progression into depth. The most striking features are the tall Sabal palms that march across the middle ground, dark crowns and upper trunks dramatically silhouetted against the colorfully striped sky, reflections of lower trunks discreetly echoing their rhythm across the foreground. The prominent public display of *The Great Florida Sunset* must have led hotel visitors to seek out smaller variations on this theme for their own homes, because the majority of Heade's Florida landscapes include many of the elements found in the big painting (plates 1, 5, 8, 9).

The strong emphasis given to the palm trees in *The Great Florida Sunset* functioned at three levels: to evoke the natural and metaphoric associations of Florida, to particularize the view of the St. Johns River, and to provide a distinctive trademark for the Flagler enterprises. Ubiquitous images of palm trees continue to this day to create a rapid shorthand linkage between Florida and Eden in every realm of visual culture. The day after the grand opening of the Ponce de Leon, the *Florida Times Union* declared that the event assured the position of St. Augustine as "the winter resort *par excellence* of America," and added that the additional planned improvements would "convert St. Augustine and its environs into as

Fig. 31. Unknown Artist. *Hotel Ponce de Leon Grounds*. 1887. From announcement of the opening of the Hotel Ponce de Leon and Alcazar, St. Augustine. Giles Litho. and Liberty Printing. Courtesy of Florida State Archives.

near an approach to the Earthly Paradise as is compatible with the cold practicalities of the modern world."[40]

The composition of tall, silhouetted cabbage palms in *The Great Florida Sunset* is quite similar in effect to the graphic moonlit *View on the Upper St. Johns River, Florida* (fig. 2, p. 4), that illustrated Edward King's *The Great South*, an important source for standard images of Florida sites. Harriet Beecher Stowe, describing a boat trip on the same stretch of the river, anticipates the pictorial use Heade would make of palms and palmettos in his Florida landscapes: "The tops of the palms rise up round in the distance as so many hay-cocks, and seeming to rise above one another as far as the eye can reach."[41] For Heade, the palm trees become ideal pictorial substitutes for the haystacks that he typically used to organize the space of his northern marsh pictures, unobtrusively measuring off the recession into depth.

Edwin Lefèvre, in his 1910 article on Flagler, noted the omnipresence of palms in the Flagler enterprises that, by that time, ranged down the entire eastern side of the state: "utilizing to the utmost this palm-*motif* are the Flagler hotels."[42] As we will see, the courtyards and gardens of Flagler's St. Augustine hotels made particularly abundant use of a variety of palm trees. Heade's *Great Florida Sunset* would have harmonized readily with the living décor to be seen all around in the spaces of the Ponce de Leon complex.

The second painting that Flagler ordered to hang as a pendant to *The Great Florida Sunset* shows, surprisingly, a non-Florida subject, *View from Fern-Tree Walk, Jamaica* (plate 6). In this case the view is even more obviously tropical and exotic than the Florida picture and much less readily accessible physically for the hotel guests than an outing on the St. Johns. We know that Heade was continuing to paint previously visited sites in the North and in the tropics even as he began to develop a complementary line of Florida themes. Perhaps Flagler was struck by the botanically specific array of unusual plants in Heade's paintings of the Caribbean and South American

Fig. 32. William Henry Jackson. *View of Alcaṛar from Roof of the Ponce de Leon Hotel*. c. 1887–89. Photograph. Detroit Publishing Company Collection. Library of Congress, Washington, D.C.

tropics and wanted a painting that would feature similar elements. Certainly this painting also would have nicely balanced the lush tropical plantings of the courtyards and gardens of the Ponce de Leon (figs. 31, 32, 33).

By commissioning these monumental landscapes, Flagler symbolically anointed Heade as "court painter" to his palatial resort. He became a steady patron, buying at least a dozen paintings from

Martin Johnson Heade in Florida

Fig. 33. William Henry Jackson. *Courtyard of the Ponce de Leon Hotel.*
c. 1887–89. Photograph. Detroit Publishing Company Collection.
Library of Congress, Washington, D.C.

Heade over the years; no other artist received such continuing support from Flagler. His purchases included every type of subject that Heade worked on during his Florida years: Florida landscapes, northeastern marshes, hummingbirds with orchids, flower paintings, and even a portrait commission.[43]

Flagler also took other measures to promulgate artistic images that would promote his St. Augustine project. He hired William

Henry Jackson, already well known for his dramatic images of the West, to photograph the hotel before it opened. Jackson had worked closely with Thomas Moran at Yellowstone and would continue to collaborate with him on later projects. Like Moran, Jackson had established close relationships with railroad and hotel promoters. Those connections enabled him to play a significant role in the codification of a repertory of visual images that would be used to advertise western destinations for tourism and development. "Jackson's southern excursions in the 1880s and 1890s helped do for Florida what his work for the railroads and government did for the West."[44]

In addition to creating "persuasive, but unspectacular" views of the hotel (see figs. 24, 28, 32, 33), Jackson devoted part of his 1887 and 1888 Flagler-sponsored campaigns to exploring the natural surroundings in Florida (figs. 34, 35).[45] The telling comments of Peter B. Hales about these photos underscore their relation to his earlier Yellowstone images:

> Battered boats peek out from around the bends of . . . [various streams] . . . surrounded by regions of silence, enigma, timelessness. How could these pictures have fit within the Gilded-Age image of the relation of man and nature? They seem anything but confirmations of Spencerian doctrines. An answer seems to lie in the forces of decay that permeate the photographs, revealing themselves in the overhanging mosses, in the huge but dying trees, in the whitened tree trunks that protrude from the

water. The overwhelming sense is of a nature both powerful and doomed. And the human figures suggest a further parallel. They are of two types: the native corresponds here, in his primitiveness and adaptation to the conditions, to the Indian of the West; and the tourist, who is rarely visible but always implied by the presence of the camera. This is nature as museum piece, as specimen—as *park*, and these pictures correspond closely to the views of Yellowstone that Jackson would make in 1892. Nature is powerful, but its power will pass; until then, we must hurry to witness its spectacular qualities.[46]

Jackson's photographs present an array of the nearby natural beauties easily accessible by steamboat excursions along the rivers and creeks of Florida. The view from the steamer compensates for some of the difficulties that might arise in photographing the dense hammock of Florida, opening up sufficient space to allow the photographer distance and perspective. Just as in Heade's paintings, the reflective surfaces of the water, the opportunities for dramatically silhouetting palm trees, and the moody atmospheric effects are all effectively exploited. Jackson also strolled through the streets near the hotel to capture on film the most picturesque street views and buildings. It is not coincidental that his repertory of images included all the standard "postcard" views of St. Augustine. Jackson was particularly anxious to create a stock of images that could be marketed to tourists as visual mementos of their trip to Florida, either as full-size display prints or as postcards.[47] Jackson's

Fig. 34. William Henry Jackson. *Bank of the St. Johns.* c. 1887–89. Photograph. Detroit Publishing Company Collection. Library of Congress, Washington, D.C.

photographs, in fact, regularly echoed subjects and general themes illustrated in King's *The Great South* and other early guidebooks. Martin Johnson Heade and other artists working in the studios at the Ponce de Leon were addressing these same subjects. Heade's attitude towards his natural subjects had many parallels to that of Jackson, with his tourist's-eye view of "nature as museum piece."

Martin Johnson Heade in Florida

Jackson's views of and from the Ponce de Leon highlight many of the artistic features of the building, but they also make clear the importance of nature in creating the overall effect of the resort. All of the images and descriptions of the hotel emphasize natural features that both surrounded it and were incorporated into its design.

Fig. 35. William Henry Jackson. *Sebastian Creek, Florida*. c. 1887–89. Photograph. Detroit Publishing Company Collection. Library of Congress, Washington, D.C.

The land acquired from Anderson to provide the site for the hotel included a large orange grove that ran between the buildings and the nearby San Sebastian salt marsh, and that was enhanced as a pleasure ground for the hotel by pathways and additional plantings. The brochure published by Carrère and Hastings before the hotel opened (see fig. 31) shows guests strolling and resting among the orange trees whose irregular forms picturesquely echo the multi-towered profile of the building. The description of the gardens is a lush one:

> In this beautiful garden one can find realized all his dreams of Southern splendor. Nothing could be more luscious than to stroll at noon under the dense canopy of the Orange Archway or Lovers' Lane. . . . But no less effective is the grove seen from the hotel windows. You look down over a sea of glossy, brilliant green, dotted thickly with golden oranges and combining richly with the deep Southern sky. But the garden is rich in other trees and flowers. What with the date-palms and palmettos, creamy magnolias and scarlet pomegranates, dainty lilies and brilliant verbenas, vines here and mosses there, the garden is a wilderness of beauty. And all this without a word about the roses! Turn the wealth of all the New York flower shops into Washington Square, and you can form some idea of what St. Augustine roses are.[48]

The brochure, which was widely distributed in both the United States and Europe to advertise the opening of the hotel, also comments on the beautifully landscaped terrace on the roof of the hotel, easily accessible by elevator, "a unique garden sixty feet above the court!" From the roof terrace, visitors could get the elevated view so rare in this flat country: "The view takes in the sea, the town, the gardens, and the Florida wilderness that creeps up to the very door of St. Augustine."[49] William Henry Jackson took advantage of this prospect to create sweeping views of St. Augustine from the hotel roof (see fig. 32).

Guests of the Ponce de Leon usually arrived at the railroad station newly built by Flagler near the San Sebastian River to accommodate the lines he had acquired in order to provide the most efficient and luxurious service for visitors. They then traveled by carriage to the front gateway of the hotel where they were dropped off while their luggage continued around to the back. They could look across an elaborately designed palm-studded plaza to the less expensive but equally exotic-looking Alcazar Hotel (see fig. 32) that had been built as an annex to the Ponce de Leon, and then pass through the gates and the tropical garden courtyard to the main entrance and reception area. This Fountain Court (see fig. 33) was perhaps the most memorable blending of nature and artifice incorporated into the hotel complex. Two paved pathways intersected at the center of a 150-foot square; each ended at one of the entrances, and all converged on a central fountain. The fountain, colorfully decorated with tiles and ceramic frogs and turtles, was surely

meant to evoke the Fountain of Youth. The entire ensemble, with its symmetrical beds of palms and roses and other flowers, conforms to an iconography of paradise gardens that reaches back to the Middle Ages and perhaps even beyond. The mastery with which the hotel laid out all of its tricks of nature and art to soothe and seduce the tourist is succinctly, and a bit sardonically, captured in Henry James's 1907 description of his visit to the scene:

> The Ponce de Leon, for that matter, comes as near producing, all by itself, the illusion of romance as a highly modern, a most cleverly-constructed and smoothly-administered great modern caravansary can come; it is largely "in the Moorish style" (as the cities of Spain preserve the record of that manner); it breaks out, on every pretext, into circular arches and embroidered screens, into courts and cloisters, arcades and fountains, fantastic projections and lordly towers, and is, in all sorts of ways and in the highest sense of the word, the most "amusing" of hotels. It did for me, at St. Augustine, I was well aware, everything that an hotel can do.[50]

Jackson's photographs and the early engravings of the hotel thoroughly bear out this impression, and both played a significant role in advertising the wonders of the Ponce de Leon to a widely dispersed public.

By far the most elaborate project to enlist art as a promoter of tourism was the series of seven artists' studios erected by Flagler

Fig. 36. *Artists' Studios at the Ponce de Leon Hotel.* c. 1887–92. Photograph. Courtesy of St. Augustine Historical Society.

egant and cultured tone designed to attract rich patrons who saw artistic interests as enhancing their status. In turn, the artists would create images of Florida and St. Augustine that would circulate an appealing image of the area among wealthy northerners who might be drawn to pay their own visits to the scenes.

The idea of artists-in-residence at a luxury hotel had precedents in other tourist areas, particularly the White Mountains of New Hampshire, and some of the artists who came to St. Augustine divided their time with such northern venues. We have noted that the hotel manager's brother, George Seavey, traveled back and forth to the Maplewood Hotel in New Hampshire according to the season. Frank Shapleigh, another New Englander, continued to serve as artist-in-residence at one of the largest and grandest of the White Mountain hotels in the summer while he occupied one of the Ponce de Leon studios for the winter season. The one-room studio building constructed for Shapleigh next to Crawford House at Crawford's Notch, New Hampshire, was described by *Scribner's Monthly* as "so picturesque and attractive that it is one of the sights of the place."[52] Such successful precedents were certainly an important inspiration to Flagler, and his decision to include not one but seven artists' studios was thoroughly in keeping with the unstinting extravagance of every aspect of his project.

Heade was delighted with the prospect of being one of the first occupants of these studios and announced to Loomis that he would

on the grounds of the hotel (fig. 36). A contemporary newspaper gives this account: "When Mr. Flagler built the Hotel Ponce de Leon, among other sensible things he did about that time, in connection with the appointments of this public palace, he built another building, not quite so big, it is true, as the Ponce de Leon, but big enough to comfortably ensconce a score or more of artists in *ateliers* of a kind to delight the eyes of a Meissonier or a Fortuny."[51] Flagler recognized that the artists' presence would add to the el-

move into the Ponce de Leon studio for "the season" although he already had two studios at his home in North City. "Among other things to please the hotel guests," he wrote, "Flagler has put up a row of studios . . . adjoining the hotel, and they are taken already. Two Boston artists [George Seavey and Shapleigh], German [a St. Augustine resident who specialized in miniature portraits], and 'me too' have taken our share."[53]

The studios were housed in a long two-story concrete building at the rear of the hotel. The lower story contained storage rooms and may have been a stable at one time. A continuous columned balcony ran along the upper story, harmonizing the design with the rest of the hotel and providing an open-air corridor connecting the studios. Alternating with concrete supports were columns formed of palm trunks, a detail found in some early St. Augustine buildings and one that nicely blends the building with the palm-filled landscape around it. The interiors of the studios were spacious and well-lighted, with skylights in addition to both north and south windows. The dividing walls between the studios were built of wood, covered in canvas, and painted. Each studio had its own fireplace.[54]

The furnishings of the individual studios were self-consciously selected, as the rooms were used not only as working spaces, but also as showrooms and salons. These rooms carried on the taste for elaborately appointed studios that had become established in venues such as New York's Tenth Street Studio Building and that

reached its apogee in the last quarter of the nineteenth century.[55] Interiors filled with antiques and exotic knick-knacks created a milieu in which the artist appeared as a gentleman (or gentlewoman), a genius both cultured and gifted in the manner of the artists of the Renaissance. The studio was more than a work space; it became a theatrical setting in which the artist enacted a role designed to disguise the necessary role of commerce in art, as described by Sarah Burns:

> The opulently bedecked studio, which was both a store and not a store and yet in every sense a showroom, answered (for a time at least) the need for artists to draw attention to themselves without creating the appearance of being crass retailers or advertising men. The studio interior was of course no conventional emporium designed for effective mass marketing. Most of the things there, all the bits and pieces of the collection, were not literally for sale. Their job was to produce an art atmosphere to make the place attractive and to advertise both producer and product. One writer discerned this, noting that the bric-à-brac and the studio were the ambitious painter's "properties," designed to "aid in bringing him customers and raising his prices." Most, however, chose not to highlight this function, tending instead to celebrate the studio as temple of art, shrine to taste, or haunt of genius. This in itself testifies to the success of the strategy.[56]

Visitors to the St. Augustine studios were as likely to comment on the décor and the social milieu as on the artwork. A Jacksonville

Martin Johnson Heade in Florida

reporter, visiting the studios shortly after the opening of the Hotel Ponce de Leon, declared George Seavey's atelier "a gem of art," and went on to state, "it would take an artist to properly describe it."[57] Despite this reservation, the reviewer proceeded to provide a rich catalog of studio trappings that included costly Turkish rugs, gold-embroidered Japanese tapestries, peacock-feather fans from India, and painted saints from Europe, along with a plethora of other exotic odds and ends. A few years later Seavey's studio still stood out as the most lavish in the row. The reviewer from the *Tatler* described it as "artistic and beautiful" and adds that "draperies, hangings, Venetian vases, bric-a-brac form a harmonious whole, fitting resting place for the beautiful products of his brain and hands."[58] Shapleigh's rooms were notable for their "quaint old piano and cabinets . . . delightful pictures and pretty decorations," and a visitor to his studio was likely to find "so many articles of interest besides the pictures that a visit to it is apt to exceed the regulation length."[59] The chief attractions in Martin Johnson Heade's quarters were the exquisite works of art that surrounded the veteran artist, and fewer comments appear on the other accoutrements of the studio. The "dean of the studios" was himself a major attraction, and he apparently entertained his guests with tales of his previous wanderings, illustrating his anecdotes with references to his pictures or to some of his exotic collections: "The veteran artist, Mr. M. J. Heade surrounded by his beautiful Florida scenery, with

their beautiful sunrises and sunsets, painting rare orchids and relating stories of his travels in their native wilds, illustrating them with his collection of butterflies gathered there; or with laughable stories of his life as an artist in the great city, while you enjoy his beautifully painted Jacqueminot roses or Cherokee or Cloth of Gold and wonder why the finish and luster of his plush used for backgrounds so far excels anything else of that kind."[60]

The ateliers became an important element of the cultural and social life of the hotel, with accounts of the receptions held there featured regularly in the local press: "The receptions tendered the public by the artists occupying the Ponce de Leon studios occur each week on Friday evening, and have been among the most enjoyable features of the season. Here young and old gathered and spent an hour in social converse among the many creations of the artists' hands, the conceptions of their brain, that are as varied in subject and treatment as it is possible to be."[61] Clearly, the art studios were an important element in creating the atmosphere of Renaissance grace and civilization that Flagler sought to sustain throughout the Ponce de Leon. The genteel note imparted to the hotel milieu was captured in the *Tatler*: "A visit to the studios is like exchanging one's innermost thoughts with a sympathizing friend; the influence is felt for days after."[62] The cultured aura fostered by the studios was part of the elaborate illusion that was all-important to the commercial success of the hotel, which charged high prices to guests who participated in the fiction of a Renaissance court. The reports on the receptions enhanced the social status of the attendees and provided abundant free advertising for the artists and for the hotel.

At times the artists must have had to struggle to sustain their roles in a charade that barely cloaked the commercial aspects of the enterprise: "A visit to the Ponce de Leon studios has become one of the features of a visit to the city. Everybody goes there; many going again and again, and many go and discuss art and artists in a manner distracting to the artists because they know nothing about the subject discussed, but the charming people who contribute so much to the pleasure of the visitors make no complaint but 'like patience on a monument, smile at criticism.'"[63]

Martin Johnson Heade was not only the artistic leader of this studio circle; he appears to have become its social leader as well. An 1891 note in the *St. Augustine News*, predecessor of the chatty *Tatler*, demonstrated the degree to which Heade had become the "big fish" in the small artistic pond of St. Augustine: "The studio of Mr. M. J. Heade is one of the favorite resorts of the city, not only on account of the beautiful reproductions of flowers and field to be found there, but on account of Mr. Heade's social popularity, who, together with his wife, make a social center for the city."[64] Although Heade was a permanent resident of St. Augustine and was regularly sending work to northern dealers, he gladly seized the opportunity to become one of the first tenants of "Artists' Row," as the studio complex was soon dubbed. When the hotel reopened each January, he regularly "abandoned his picturesque studio in the grounds of his lovely home in North City, and moved most of his treasures into No. 7, of the Ponce de Leon studios, that his friends and patrons [might] have less difficulty in finding him."[65]

Heade had recognized the advantages of this sort of collective studio arrangement from the time of his long affiliation with the Tenth Street Studio Building. Those advantages were collegial and social but also very much commercial. The artists of the Ponce de Leon studio produced and displayed their wares with the hope of selling them to the wealthy hotel guests, and they chose subjects that would also help to further the reputation of Flagler's hotel as a cultural enterprise. Ellen Robbins gives a vivid picture of the atmosphere of these studios, in her "Reminiscences of a Flower Painter." She herself stayed at the more modest Barcelona Hotel but frequently stopped in on her friend in the Flagler hotel:

Mrs. K—was a fine watercolor painter, and charming in her conversation. She had a studio, one of many built by Mr. Flagler, and it was very pleasant to drop in on her and see her pictures. On Friday evening of each week the studios were open to the public. One had a good opportunity in these receptions of seeing the people who went for the winter to St. Augustine,—some very interesting, but a large number so uninteresting that it was depressing. The artists were very eager to sell their pictures; and these Flagler studios all being in a row, with a flight of stairs at each end,—when any one looking like a buyer came by a door, a head was quickly protruded to see what artist was fortunate enough to secure the same. Boarding at the Ponce de Leon was considered a wise thing, no matter how poor the artist, because there one was most likely to meet the rich people.[66]

The commercial effectiveness of the studios was attested by regular reports in the *Tatler* of the successful sales completed by the artists.

As the oldest and most established of the studio painters, Heade must have been looked up to by the younger artists, none of whom ever equaled his reputation or matched the individuality and quality of his work. Although Heade is now accorded a status considerably elevated above his nearly forgotten St. Augustine colleagues, his choices of subject and approach were often quite in keeping with these other studio artists. In fact, examining the sorts of subjects that were fostered by the St. Augustine studios, and how these worked into the promotional agenda of the hotel enterprise, may provide some new insights into the work that Heade did in this final stage in his career.

In 1998, Sandra Barghini organized the most comprehensive modern look at the work of the St. Augustine Art Colony for the Flagler Museum, appropriately housed in Flagler's Palm Beach mansion, Whitehall. The exhibition catalog provides a good overview of the artists who worked in the Ponce de Leon studios as well as a few who did not. Several generalizations can be made about the work seen in the studios. Many of the artists (including Heade) offered some work done elsewhere or at least representing other places. Heade continued to paint northern marshes and hummingbird and orchid paintings with South American backdrops, but increasingly he added Florida subjects and greatly expanded his production of flower paintings. F. Arthur Callender, a painter of both genre and landscape, seems to have exhibited mostly scenes of Louisiana, the subject for which he was best known. Felix de Crano (fig. 50, p. 89), like Heade, produced mostly landscape and flower paintings in Florida, but he also displayed an additional roomful of European subjects. William Staples Drown painted the same standard picturesque scenes of St. Augustine photographed by Jackson; Frank Shapleigh (fig. 37) depicted many of the same scenes and displayed them alongside his New England views. George Seavey (fig. 38) seems to have painted flower pictures almost exclusively, whereas both Ellen Robbins and Laura Woodward (fig. 39) alternated between floral pieces and landscapes, as did Heade.[67]

The local scenes, especially the most identifiable views, seem to have been predictably popular with tourists. "The St. Augustine painters," writes historian Frederic A. Sharf, "traveled the same routes that the tourists took, going down the St. Johns River to Ocklawaha. . . . They provided the tourist with paintings covering

Fig. 37. Frank Shapleigh. *Panorama of the City of St. Augustine and the Castillo San Marco.* 1886. Oil on canvas. 22 × 36 in. From the collection of the Museum of Arts and Sciences, Daytona Beach, Florida. Gift of Kenneth Worcester Dow and Mary Mohan Dow.

all aspects of his St. Augustine vacation." Sharf goes on to note "Travelers from all over the country bought pictures of St. Augustine, and those not sold on the spot were offered in Boston, New York, or Philadelphia by art dealers and at auction galleries. Eventually such Florida scenes became familiar throughout the country, largely owing to the activity of the St. Augustine artists' colony." [68] The artists who concentrated on the predictable set of images of the standard shrines of Florida tourism usually preferred to include prominent man-made features, since Florida's natural landscape lacked the readily recognizable mountains or waterfalls or rock formations that marked the sites of tourist pilgrimage notable in the rest of the country. They also tended to enliven their scenery with genre details. Heade, on the other hand, kept his views generalized and even seemed to embrace the rather generic qualities of the landscape. He wrote to Loomis, "As the St. Johns River scenery is perfectly flat—as it is here—I have neglected the northern meadows lately & taken to Florida."[69] Heade's landscapes were sufficiently descriptive of the Florida tourist experience to be easily marketable emblems of the state, although they avoided the ploys adopted by his fellow studio artists to underscore their picturesque qualities. The enduring powers of Heade's paintings to elevate, at least metaphorically, his chosen vistas of flat riverbank and marsh will be the subject of the final chapter.

St. Augustine and Flagler seem to have embraced Heade as *their*

Fig. 38. George Seavey. *Snowballs.* Undated. Oil on canvas. 19 × 27 in. Flagler College, St. Augustine, Florida.

painter. There was even a plan to have him represent the state of Florida at the World's Columbian Exposition in Chicago in 1893. A proposal set forth in the *Tatler* suggested that both the landscapes and the floral paintings of Heade would be perfect choices to convey the image of the state in this national forum: "Mr. M. J. Heade has adopted St. Augustine as his home, has painted charming pictures of the rivers, lakes, beautiful hammocks of the State, has made a study of the atmospheric effects—of the sunrises and

Fig. 39. Laura Woodward. *Royal Poinciana Blossoms.* c. 1890s. Watercolor on paper. 12 × 17 in. Henry Morrison Flagler Museum, Palm Beach, Florida. © Flagler Museum.

afterglows. Would not a collection of his pictures be interesting to every visitor to the Florida building? Is it quite fair to the State to allow these to grace other exhibitions? Mr. Heade's studies of flowers peculiar to the State would be another attraction that the State cannot forego."[70]

"Studies of flowers peculiar to the State" were one of Heade's major endeavors in the Florida years. He had begun to develop his skills and reputation as a painter of floral still life more than twenty years earlier at the same time that he was becoming established as a landscape painter. Indeed, his simultaneous in-depth exploration of these two different genres was unique among the artists of his day. If we set aside the hummingbird and orchid pictures, however, the flower pictures constitute a somewhat minor fraction of his pre-Florida production. In Florida the proportions of flower paintings to landscapes is nearly reversed, and the artist also invented entirely new types in this genre. The Florida flower pieces, especially the paintings of magnolias, have been the works most recently "rediscovered" by Heade's modern admirers, and they received their apotheosis in the display and critical response accorded them in the millennial exhibition. Previous considerations of these paintings, however, have somewhat glossed over the specific circumstances of their production and reception. The following chapter will explore the special significance of these floral works in their Florida context.

CHAPTER THREE

Mementos from the "Land of Flowers"

EADE'S INTENSE LOVE OF FLOWERS is abundantly evident in his surviving correspondence. When visiting at a seaside villa in Brazil, he voluntarily took on the chore of providing a daily flower arrangement: "it is a task imposed on me—principally self imposed, but by custom grown into a sort of duty—to gather and 'fix' a beautiful bouquet for the breakfast table; and we often indulge in two or three."[1] His letters to Eben Loomis regularly referred to whatever seasonal flowers were blooming, and he reminisced about mutual rambles in search of the delicate trailing arbutus that he had tried unsuccessfully to grow in his new home: "It refuses to have anything to do with Florida, if it is the land of flowers!"[2] Church addressed him facetiously as "Martin Johnson Heade, Flour Painter," and regularly reported to him on the status of the flowering fruit trees at his Hudson River estate, Olana. One year, when the apple trees had put on a particularly impressive show, he lamented that Heade did not have the opportunity to "come up and appleblossomate for a few days."[3] Heade frequently exchanged specimens and seeds of flowering plants and unusual botanical varieties with both of these correspondents.

In St. Augustine, Heade could gratify his love of flowers all year, and indulge his taste for gardening as well (figs. 25, p. 45; 40). Visitors were enchanted by his "orange and oleander and jasmine embowered home."[4] He found a ready market for painted souvenirs from "the land of flowers." In the final decade of his life, flower paintings appear to have formed a greater and greater percentage of his output, to judge from the annual descriptions of his studio contents. A visitor to the Ponce de Leon studios in 1896 would have found this spectacle in Heade's atelier: "Mr. Heade, assisted by Mrs. Heade, received most cordially, surrounded by the exquisite blossoms Mr. Heade loves to paint, great Jacquminot [sic] roses, rich and full, their more modest sisters, the fine Cherokee rose, and the magnolia, lotus and orchids, around them. Mr. Heade has fewer landscapes on exhibition than usual, evidently flowers, that he loves so well, are occupying his time entirely."[5]

The geometric increase in Martin Johnson Heade's production of flower paintings during his Florida years fits the general picture of production and patronage in the Ponce de Leon studios. Lesser lights of "Artists' Row" also found flower painting profitable. George Seavey, brother of the hotel manager, was, if we judge by the reports in the newspapers, one of the most popular of the studio painters. By 1888, a Jacksonville paper noted that Seavey's "genius has long been appreciated by Mr. Flagler, who is the possessor of no less than seven of his pictures, three of which occupy positions of honor in the parlors of the Ponce de Leon, while others adorn the walls of Mr. Flagler's private residence in New York."[6] The paintings were still exciting admiration in 1891, when the *St. Augustine News* noted that Seavey's flower images in the parlors "received more attention and praise on opening day than any there."[7] In 1893, Seavey was so busy that the *Tatler* gave this report: "Mr. George Seavey usually spends his time here resting and showing his beautiful flower pictures; this season he has been obliged to work in order to supply orders and have a number on hand, so highly is his work appreciated."[8]

Like fellow New Englanders Frank Shapleigh and William Staples Drown, with whom he shared many common associations, Seavey began as a landscape painter. However, he seems to have

Fig. 40. *Heade Sitting Indoors, St. Augustine.* c. 1900. Photograph. St. Augustine *Tatler,* March 4, 1905, p. 17. Courtesy of St. Augustine Historical Society.

concentrated almost entirely on flower paintings by the time he began to winter in St. Augustine. Seavey's skillful if uninspired floral offerings (fig. 38, p. 67) were clearly popular and successful sellers with his tourist clientele in both the North and the South. His regular sales to Flagler and others probably encouraged Heade to step up his own production of flower painting.

Occupying studios at opposite ends of "Artists' Row," Seavey and Heade also offered stylistic alternatives "as different as possible, Mr. Heade working out all the delicate tracery of leaf and petal, while Mr. Seavey secures his effects so brilliant and artistic by massing quantities of flowers and painting them broadly."[9] Heade

Martin Johnson Heade in Florida

clung to his meticulous realism in the face of changing fashions at the end of the century, and his skill and tenacity continued to elicit admiration from the St. Augustine audience. The *Tatler* regularly praised Heade's flower paintings for their "wonderful fidelity and truth," and commended his "careful, painstaking work."[10] His steady production of floral works was a logical response to the popularity of these subjects with the buying public, as Stebbins acknowledges: "With regard to the flowers, we can surmise that he would keep a sampling of his wares on his walls, like any good businessman; then if a rose, a daisy composition, or something else were sold, he would doubtless paint a similar picture to replace it. Heade's Florida patrons apparently wanted highly realistic still lifes, and he did his best to comply: the *Tatler* commented in 1897, '[Heade] belongs to the Raphaelite school of painting, doing painstaking, conscientious work.'"[11]

While working in New England, Seavey had probably already discovered that flower paintings were a popular item for resort visitors, but the commercial success of such motifs in St. Augustine is particularly easy to understand. After all, what could be a more appropriate souvenir of Florida, whose very name evoked the "land of flowers"? The range of Heade's floral still lifes in St. Augustine clearly indicates that his choices of species were increasingly tailored to evoke Florida and, in some cases, to make specific references to the city and to the Flagler hotel complex.

Laura Woodward, another artist closely tied to the Flagler enterprises, also used specific flower species to create place associations. Woodward had already visited St. Augustine several times when she decided to move there in 1893. She traveled and painted in many locales along the east coast and was credited by the *Tatler* with introducing visitors to the range and variety of Florida scenes from Anastasia Island down to Lake Worth. "Her pictures," declares the reviewer, "have been a great benefit to the State in making its characteristics known to purchasers in all parts of the land."[12] She liked Lake Worth (now Palm Beach) so well that she decided to move there permanently in 1894, and she is supposed to have influenced Flagler's decision to expand his enterprises to the southern part of the state. She soon established her studio at his new Hotel Royal Poinciana, and she took advantage of the hotel's name to create her most successful pictures, images of the flame-red blooms of the royal poinciana tree (fig. 39, p. 68). Maybelle Mann's recent (1999) history of art in Florida gives this account: "Her constant press centered on her studies of the royal poinciana tree with its magnificent red flowers. . . . Since the flower blooms only during the summer, her paintings were the only means by which many winter visitors were able to see the blossoms. Woodward's paintings, a source of great local pride, sold nationally."[13]

Heade's floral selections, although slightly less obvious than the trademark royal poinciana chosen by Woodward, were also meant to convey quite specific local associations to a national audience. Five flower species are featured in the majority of Heade's surviving Florida still lifes: roses (see fig. 43), Cherokee roses (plate 12; see fig. 46), orange blossoms (see fig. 45), magnolias (plate 11; see fig. 48), and lotus flowers (plate 13). He developed new compositional formats for rendering these blooms and typically concentrated on a single species in each painting. There are also three paintings of yellow daisies (or marguerites) as well as several one-time experiments. The surviving single paintings of Japanese plums, nasturtiums, and laurel blossoms have all been passed down from members of Heade's immediate family, suggesting either that they were mementos painted to please special personal requests or preferences or that they did not sell successfully to the general audience and thus remained in the family after his death.[14] Pink oleanders and yellow jessamine, or jasmine (see fig. 49), were also the subjects of unique known paintings, although the studio reviews suggest that Heade must have painted the jasmine rather frequently.[15]

In the 1860s and 1870s, Heade had painted mixed bouquets in elaborate vases (fig. 41) and had accompanied them with various other still life elements, including books, jewel boxes, strings of pearls, and hatpins. Most are set against bare walls, but a few appear in front of curtains or elaborately patterned wallpaper. The vases may be set on highly polished wood surfaces that allow the artist to show off his virtuosity in rendering reflections, or they feature fringed, lacy, or elaborately brocaded table coverings. Only roses and apple blossoms are occasionally shown without vases, and these two types are also sometimes completely removed from the parlor interior and moved into the mixed genre category of the orchid, hummingbird, and passion flower paintings which combine close-up flowers with distant sky or landscape. Orchids and apple blossoms continue to appear among Heade's Florida work, and in many cases we know that he copied the blooms from oil sketches that he brought south with him (fig. 42). A group of twenty-four oil sketches was given to Miss Wilma Davis, who gave them to the St. Augustine Historical Society in 1944.[16] Some of these are as early as 1871, and they continue into the Florida period. Studying them in relation to the paintings provides interesting insights into Heade's working methods.

Heade often painted roses during his days in the Tenth Street Studio in New York. In many cases the rose paintings fall into closely related groupings, as in a succession of ten (or more) paintings showing single or multiple blooms in crystal glasses done in the five years before the move to Florida.[17] This group showcases Heade's favorite rose, the lush, deep red Général Jacqueminot, sometimes colloquially known as "General Jacks." The "plain glass tumblers" that complement the roses so exquisitely were, as Stebbins has observed, sought-after items of the growing consumer

Fig. 41. (*left*) Martin Johnson Heade. *Mixed Flowers in a Silver Vase*. c. 1871–80. Oil on artist's board. 18 × 10¼ in. Henry Morrison Flagler Museum, Palm Beach, Florida. © Flagler Museum.

Fig. 42. (*above*) Martin Johnson Heade. *Study of* Lealia Purpurata *and Another Orchid*. c. 1870. Oil on canvas (unstretched). 8½ × 13 in. Courtesy of St. Augustine Historical Society.

culture: "Though the tumblers appear ordinary to modern eyes, they too were upscale items popular among the middle class. Such glasses were advertised as 'tumbler half pints' by numerous firms; they are made of blown glass with diamond-shaped etching over a frosted area, with cut flat flutes below."[18] In Florida, Heade recapitulated this series in a more baroque vein, bunching together as many as half-a-dozen buds and half-open blooms, adding plush draperies, and experimenting with more varied and dramatic lighting (fig. 43). Henry Flagler owned at least two of these paintings.[19]

Such closely related series, with their subtly nuanced variations of composition and lighting, suggest to contemporary minds a very modern or even postmodern practice, but one suspects that Heade was largely motivated by discovering a readily saleable subject. The numbers of a given subject were undoubtedly directly related to their popularity with Heade's customers, and this factor must have been even more important in the Florida years, as the artist came to rely more and more on direct sales from his studio. He continued to favor the crimson Jacqueminot and to regularly exaggerate its intense color. He was undaunted by one art critic's comment that this popular rose was not "an artist's flower . . . [but] only a society flower," or the further note that this particular species "has only held its place so long because even fashion likes to get a good deal of size and a good deal of scent for its money."[20] The clientele of the St. Augustine resorts were indubitably of the

sort that liked a good deal of size and scent for their money, and Heade seems to have been more than willing to indulge that taste. An 1891 reviewer notes his pleasure at a visitor's "request to see some 'Jack roses,'" and affirms the ready marketability of this subject, adding that "no doubt by this time the enquirer for them is their proud possessor."[21]

Roses made particularly appropriate souvenirs of St. Augustine in general and the Hotel Ponce de Leon in particular. Northern visitors were sometimes disappointed that, in January, they did not always find Florida as blossom-filled as its name implied, but they were delighted with the splendid roses in the gardens and courtyards of the Flagler hotels. A Canadian visitor concludes a descriptive letter to the Toronto paper: "I can fancy nothing pleasanter than to be able to spend the summers in Canada and the winters just here in this beautiful, quaint old place, with its roses, and such roses, blooming all the winter through."[22] The frontispiece of the engraved brochure announcing the hotel opening depicts well-dressed tourists gathered at the Ladies Entrance from the Ponce de Leon courtyard (fig. 44). The image is overlaid by a pair of enormous roses, underlining the special link of the blooms to St. Augustine and to the hotel. A few days before the much-awaited grand opening on January 12, 1888, a Jacksonville paper reported that the famous St. Augustine roses were doing their part to add to the splendor of the occasion: "St. Augustine glories in her beautiful

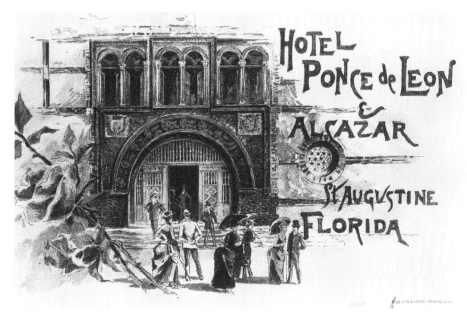

Fig. 43. (*left*) Martin Johnson Heade. *Red Roses and Rose Buds in a Glass*. c. 1883–1900. Oil on canvas. 24 × 15 in. Courtesy of The R. W. Norton Art Gallery, Shreveport, Louisiana.

Fig. 44. (*above*) Unknown artist. *Hotel Ponce de Leon and Alcazar*. From announcement of the opening of the Hotel Ponce de Leon and Alcazar, 1887. Giles Litho. and Liberty Printing. Courtesy of Florida State Archives.

roses. Nowhere in the South are these beautiful flowers cultivated with greater success. They bloom continuously all the year round, but at certain seasons, of course, are more plentiful than others. The present beautiful weather is hurrying the buds out in great profusion, and on the opening of the Ponce de Leon on Thursday the rose trees will be loaded with a wealth of bloom."[23]

Visitors seem to have been equally delighted with the painted roses they found in Heade's studio (see fig. 43). The reviews in the *Tatler* regularly mention these rose paintings, and the Jacqueminot features in virtually every list of his studio contents. Descriptions of studio visits in 1894 also mention "a cluster of Marie van Hautes resting against a plush background of softest green harmonizing with the leaves and petals of the flower," and elsewhere Cloth of Gold and Marechal Neil roses are included in the catalog of Heade's floral subjects.[24] Marechal Neil roses were prominently featured in the Fountain Court through which every visitor entered the Hotel Ponce de Leon.[25]

Many of the Florida rose paintings continued to show the blossoms in elegant vases and crystal glasses, but Heade also employed a new type of composition that seems to belong strictly to his Florida period. The format changes from the vertical one favored for flowers in containers to a horizontal one, and the cut flowers are placed, seemingly casually, on a velvet tablecloth. The horizontal table edge precisely halves the composition. The more or less crumpled, variously colored plush contrasts with a neutral barely textured wall, and the thorny stems and leaves contrast with the voluptuous petals of the roses. Compositionally, this format combined the exaggerated horizontality and the delicate orchestration of light and color that characterized Heade's luminist landscape paintings. The casually displayed blossoms are at once more sensual and more fragile than the formal arrangements in containers. Without water, the already fleeting life span of these roses will be even briefer.

Another flower that northern visitors would be thrilled to see and to smell when they arrived at the Ponce de Leon in January was the fragrant orange blossom. The land Flagler purchased included extensive orange groves that became the pleasure grounds of the hotel (fig. 31, p. 55). Visitors wandering in the groves in the early part of the season might find "flower and fruit growing amicably together on sister boughs," as noted in the promotional brochure for Flagler's hotels.[26] As they still do today, tourists regularly shipped oranges north to their friends, and an advertisement in the *Tatler* urged them to send the aromatic blossoms as well: "The delicious fragrance of orange blossoms that fills the air can be enjoyed by friends at home. You have only to leave your order at Unico . . . and boxes of the sweet blossoms, packed with care, will be sent wherever you wish."[27] Like many transplanted northerners, Heade took great pride and pleasure in his own citrus trees, and he sent

Martin Johnson Heade in Florida

Fig. 45. Martin Johnson Heade. *Two Oranges with Orange Blossoms*. c. 1883–95. Oil on canvas. 12 × 20⅛ in. Collection of Diane and Blaine Fogg. Photograph courtesy of Sotheby's, Inc. © 2002.

regular reports to his friend Eben Loomis on the vicissitudes of his orange crop.[28]

Painted representations of both fruit and flowers could provide a less fragrant but more durable memento of one's sojourn in Florida. Heade created half a dozen known paintings of orange blossoms (fig. 45): two are vertical views of flowers in crystal tumblers, and the other four use the new horizontal composition, with boughs casually laid on a table. All but one of the horizontal compositions include fruit along with the flowers; tables are both bare and covered. The orange blossom paintings are regularly mentioned in the descriptions of studio visits, but perhaps they did not sell as rapidly as the cultured roses, Cherokee roses, and magnolias that, judging from the surviving numbers, must have been Heade's most sought-after subjects.

Unlike the pampered Jacqueminots and Marechal Neils, Cherokee roses grew wild in the southern states in the nineteenth century. In addition to several oil sketches, there are eighteen oil paintings of Cherokee roses (plate 12, fig. 46) among Heade's known works.[29] The reporter from the *St. Augustine News* who visited the studios in 1891 admired many new flower compositions but was especially struck by one study of Cherokee roses, "beautiful beyond comparison, the glossy leaves, creamy white petals with their shiny surface, were depicted with such truthfulness, such attention to detail that it is hard to realize they may not be picked and worn."[30] The reviewer

for the *Tatler* in 1898 admired Heade's images of "the Cherokee rose that grows so profusely here, climbing over stumps and hedges, transforming them into things of beauty." The flowers are described as "wonderfully like; the pure white petals, yellow stamens, and glossy, dark leaves are so natural as to deceive."[31] Heade painted these striking flowers in vases and glasses and in the casual horizontal arrangements (plate 12, fig. 46) he had also adopted for cultivated roses and orange blossoms. Similarly, they appear against bare walls, on glossy reflective tables, or against plush cloths.

The success of Heade's Cherokee roses could readily be explained on aesthetic grounds alone: he is superbly sensitive to the possible mutations of lighting and composition. He made direct studies of the blooms in oil sketches (fig. 46), then used these to develop sequences of paintings that read like a set of deft variations upon an eloquent musical theme (plate 12). The popularity of the subject must have led him to regularly replenish the images on the walls of his studio, where they inspired admiring comments from visitors. Paintings of Cherokee roses would have been particularly apt souvenirs of the Flagler hotels, for the flowers were featured repeatedly in descriptions of the hotel and the activities of its visitors. To underscore the association of the flower with St. Augustine, the opening announcement for the hotel complex shows a vignette of the Old City Gates surrounded by Cherokee roses, roses, and tiny jasmine blossoms (fig. 47).

Martin Johnson Heade in Florida

Fig. 46. Martin Johnson Heade. *Branches of Cherokee Roses*. c. 1884–90. Oil on canvas (unstretched). 12 × 9 in.
Courtesy of St. Augustine Historical Society.

When Commodore George Dewey, the "hero of Manila Bay," stayed at the hotel in 1900, a highlight of the festivities was an elaborate garden party held in the orange grove. The description of this affair relates, "the background was a perfect wilderness of Cherokee roses that was very picturesque and effective."[32] In other parts of the hotel complex the Cherokees were deliberately cultivated and combined with more refined species. In the Fountain Court they were included in the elaborate mixed plantings that drew so much admiration from visitors.[33]

Fig. 47. Unknown artist. *Old City Gate*. From announcement of the opening of the Hotel Ponce de Leon and Alcazar, 1887. Giles Litho. and Liberty Printing. Courtesy of Florida State Archives.

Ellen Robbins also painted Cherokee roses while in St. Augustine, and the charming story she tells in "Reminiscences of a Flower Painter" indicates that they were plentiful in the plaza between the Ponce de Leon and the Alcazar: "The beautiful flowers I can never forget; from the beginning of March it was one continual feast. The Cherokee roses covering the piazza of Richard Dale (Mr. Flagler's gardener) were a pleasure to look at. Mr. Dale brought [them] to my room at the Barcelona, his arms full of long trailing branches of this beautiful rose, for me to paint. I found a dear little chameleon in the branches, and kept him for a pet till I left, the middle of April."[34]

Both Robbins and Felix de Crano painted watercolors of Cherokee roses. De Crano's compositions, casually placed clusters in horizontal formats, reflect the direct influence of Heade.[35] Heade himself had only to reach out the window of his cottage to find subjects for portraits of this favorite flower—although the flowers are not in bloom when the picture was taken, a photograph of the artist in the window of his St. Augustine home shows the walls overrun with the climbing roses (see fig. 40).

The reports in the *Tatler* regularly mention magnolias among the flower species gracing the walls of Heade's studio but do not single them out for any particular notice. Heade does not seem to have sent any magnolia paintings to exhibitions outside St. Augustine, although he regularly showed roses, Cherokee roses, and

Martin Johnson Heade in Florida

orchids in New York and in Worcester and Springfield, Massachu-setts and other northern venues during his Florida years.[36] Modern critics, on the other hand, have regularly selected the magnolias (plate 11, fig. 48) for extravagant praise. In 1996, for instance, Timothy Eaton describes them as "M. J. Heade's final, and argu-ably greatest series of paintings." He goes on to assert, "His paint-ings of magnolia blossoms are unique in art history having no pre-cedent or sequent in American, European, or even Oriental art."[37] The impressive group of magnolia paintings displayed in the 1999–2000 exhibition accorded this subject something of an apo-theosis. Recent critiques of the magnolia paintings would un-doubtedly be as startling to Heade and his contemporaries as the fact that a long-unknown version unearthed in an Arizona garage sale would quickly be resold for the record-breaking price of $2 million.[38]

As much or more than the orchid paintings, the magnolias have prompted extravagant psychoanalytic and sexualized readings. John Baur, who played such an important role in the modern redis-covery of Heade when he proclaimed the newly identified strain of "Luminism," is also responsible for a suggestive reading of the magnolias that subsequent authors have found irresistible. His 1954 catalog essay for an exhibition of the Karolik Collection described Heade as "obsessed, to judge from the many times he treated the subject, with the fleshy whiteness of magnolia blossoms startlingly

arrayed on sumptuous red velvet like odalisques on a couch."[39] For the last half-century, modern and postmodern critics have embroi-dered Baur's reading, so that Roberta Smith's reaction to the group of paintings encountered at the 1999–2000 retrospective seems al-most predictable: "In the final gallery, the reclining magnolia blos-soms, whose petals fall this way and that, seem to exude an aura of postcoital dishabille."[40] Writers who had projected sexual anxiety into the artist's earlier images of hummingbirds and orchids were able to find a sense of sexual fulfillment and domestic tranquility in the Florida floral paintings, as when Stebbins declares, "These pictures, more than any others, represent the painter's new feelings of comfort and well-being."[41]

Magnolias, like Cherokee roses, were instantly recognizable em-blems of the South in general and of Florida in particular. We can easily imagine that Ponce de León must have admired the large and spectacular blossoms of the magnolias that grew in particular pro-fusion along the rivers of Florida. The flowers entranced the eigh-teenth-century naturalist William Bartram as he sailed along the St. Johns River: "The Laurel Magnolias, which grow on this river, are the most beautiful and tall that I have any where seen. . . . The flow-ers are on the extremities of the subdivisions of the branches, in the center of the coronet of dark green, shining, ovate pointed entire leaves: they are large, perfectly white, and expanded like a full blown Rose. . . . The flowers of this tree are the largest and most complete yet known: when fully expanded, they are of six, eight, and nine inches in diameter."[42]

The magnificence of Florida's magnolias also drew the admiration of John Muir, later founder of the Sierra Club, as he passed through Florida in 1867 on his thousand-mile walk from Indiana to the coast of the Gulf of Mexico: "*Magnolia grandiflora* I had seen in Georgia; but its home, its better land, is here. Its large dark-green leaves, glossy bright above and rusty brown beneath, gleam and mirror the sunbeams most gloriously among countless flower-heaps of the climbing, smothering vines. It is . . . more tropical in form and expression than the orange. It speaks itself like a prince among its fellows."[43]

As development moved down the coast of Florida, nearly every community could boast a Magnolia Hotel. St. Augustine's own Magnolia Hotel, opened in the 1840s, had been the first establishment in the town pitched primarily to northern visitors. The St. Johns resort of Magnolia Springs (the name was later changed to Green Cove Springs) was the most elegant facility in eastern Florida before the Ponce de Leon, and Flagler hired the director of its Magnolia Hotel, Osborn D. Seavey, to manage his hotel complex. Indeed, magnolias were ubiquitous in place and business names, and images of the flowers were scattered across all sorts of tourist memorabilia. Descriptions of the ornamental grounds regularly mentioned the profusion of magnolias around the Hotel Ponce de Leon. Heade's choice of magnolias for a subject was therefore practically inevitable, particularly since the pictorial possibilities of the lavish blossoms perfectly suited his sensibilities. It was just as inevitable that the paintings would become popular souvenirs.

The picturesque opportunities offered by Cherokee roses and magnolias were similar: both species presented a pleasing contrast of pearly petals and glossy foliage that Heade liked to enhance by placing the flowers against richly colored plush draperies. As with the Cherokee roses, his magnolia pictures experiment with both vertical compositions that place the flowers in vases (see fig. 48) and more casual horizontal formats (plate 11). Anyone who has ever made the attempt will recognize the logistical difficulty of trying to balance the sprawling blossoms and large stiff leaves of a magnolia in a delicate upright vase, and the physical problem is matched by a visual imbalance as well. In the few paintings where Heade placed magnolias in containers, he used buds, arranged asymmetrically and echoed in shape by oval vases (see fig. 48). Fully opened blooms would clearly have overtopped and unbalanced most of the crystal tumblers or vases that Heade regularly utilized for flower paintings. So he favored the horizontal format (plate 11), and it does seem irresistible to describe these lush, blowzy flowers as "recumbent" or "reclining" on the sensuous velvet draperies that prop up the irregular blooms and foliage and provide such striking contrasts of texture and color. The aura of languor and sensuality would have been perfectly in keeping with the primary function of these paintings, which would have served as appropriate mementos of a visit to the most luxurious establishments in Florida.

It is hard to resist the thought that when Heade arrayed his blowzy magnolias against elegant plush, he may have been surreptitiously poking a bit of fun at the new rich tourists who were his potential buyers. The wild magnolias of the South are not suitable parlor flowers: their size, growth pattern, and stiff foliage make them difficult to subdue into orderly domestic flower arrangements. Harriet Beecher Stowe, who also tried to paint magnolias, described the difficulties presented by a "glorious bouquet," brought by a friend: "No ordinary flower-vase would hold it. It required a heavy stone jar, and a gallon of water; but we filled the recess of our old Franklin stove with the beauties, and the whole house was scented with their perfume."[44] The blossoms, once cut, last just a day or two, and if accidentally touched the petals will immediately turn brown. The fragility of these hearty-looking flowers might have invoked *vanitas* connotations for Heade. It also seems likely that, by placing these wild blossoms against the luxurious velvets that his buyers so much admired, he may have been

making a tongue-in-cheek comment on the difficulties of turning sows' ears into silk purses.

If magnolias were well suited to convey the sumptuous indolence of a southern vacation in the pampered ambience of the St. Augustine resorts, lotus blossoms, or water lilies, may have been even more perfectly adapted for that role (plate 13). The lotus flowers that seduced Odysseus's men into a state of blissful forgetfulness were, historically, an altogether different species, but the term "lotus" still carried connotations of sybaritic escapism. What more appropriate advertisement for the languorous entertainment proffered at the luxury resorts of St. Augustine?

The pale yellow water lily, the American lotus, grew wild in the waterways of Florida, but the flowers Heade depicted are the imported types of Oriental, or "sacred," lotus that were a popular feature of cultivated water gardens. I have not found specific references to water lily plantings in the various fountains and pools that abounded in the St. Augustine resorts of the time, but it is likely that they existed and that Heade would have found models for his specimens close at hand. His preference for the showy lotuses over other types of water lilies was probably dictated by the suggestive associations of the lotus and the effective contrast between the smooth and softly colored petals and the spiky orange and yellow corolla of the flower. The color of the petals modulates from the tenderest blush of pink on the swelling curves to a fine border of pure crimson at the edges. The play of these rosy tones against the yellow burst of the corolla recalls the delicate tonal play of the sunrises and sunsets Heade favored for so many of his Florida landscapes.

Perhaps the lotus was less popular with Heade's customers than the more characteristic magnolias and roses, because only four lotus paintings survive. Undoubtedly, as with the many paintings of the magnolias and Cherokee roses, Heade used an oil sketch as a model for all four of these works. Three of them show the same group of seven blossoms, four fully open and three buds. The open blooms are arranged so that they turn in space, supplying a three-quarter view displaying the brightly colored corolla, a profile view, and two blossoms seen from behind. The version in the Boston Museum of Fine Arts displays the bloom in three-quarter view along with a single bud set against a large leaf that curves over the flowers like an Oriental parasol.[45]

The most interesting of the lotus paintings, *Lotus Flowers: A Landscape Painting in the Background* (plate 13), provides a compressed anthology of Heade's distinctive themes, setting a floral still life against a picture-within-a-picture of one of the artist's own landscape canvases. The painted vista depicts a northern orchard, apparently one of a series showing spring showers on blossoming fruit trees, rather than a southern wetland.[46] A delightful counterpoint is developed between the "real" flowers and the fictive landscape. The pinks of the lotuses are echoed by a blush of pink from the flowering trees to the left of the painted vista. The rippling lily pad that cradles the foreground blooms is reiterated in the flowing green of the hillside. The dark swath of drapery to the far left rhymes with the heavy rain clouds in the sky. The burst of light emerging to the right of these clouds not only illuminates the landscape but seems to spill forth from the picture within the picture to become the light source for the still life. This light imparts a soft glow to the blossoms and spreads a warm reflection across the polished surface of the table. The playful juxtaposition of levels of reality recalls the whimsy of Heade's earlier *Gremlin in the Studio* (fig. 19, p. 32). Perhaps the rainy springtime landscape was meant as a reminder of the season when tourists left their period of "lotus-eating" in the South and headed back to their northern homes. Appropriately, the painting was purchased by Flagler, who must have appreciated the subtleties of its references. In the 1970s the painting was reacquired by one of Flagler's descendents and presented to the North Carolina Museum of Art.

Stebbins catalogs a single example of a Heade portrayal of *Yellow Jasmine* (fig. 49), a small panel showing an unruly bunch of the twisting vines in a clear glass tumbler set upon a plain wooden table. The small trumpetlike yellow blooms and the pointed, glossy oval leaves of the jasmine were not particularly showy, but the flower that southerners preferred to call "yellow jessamine" was

Fig. 48. (*left*) Martin Johnson Heade. *Two Magnolia Blossoms in a Glass Vase*. c. 1883–1900. Oil on canvas. 24 × 15 in. Morris Museum of Art, Augusta, Georgia.

Fig. 49. (*right*) Martin Johnson Heade. *Yellow Jasmine*. c. 1883–86. Oil on mahogany panel. 13 × 8¾ in. Private collection. Photograph courtesy of Bernard and S. Dean Levy, Inc., New York City.

much beloved for its fragrance. Surely, Heade painted many more depictions of this flower, and perhaps they have not come to light because the subject is not as widely associated with him as are the more flamboyant magnolias and Cherokee roses. In the 1890s, *Tatler* reviewers spotted "a study of yellow jasimine [*sic*] in a carafe surrounded by gold in relief," "a spray of yellow jasmine," and "several studies of yellow jasmine."[47]

Like other flowers favored by Heade, the yellow jessamine was popular in St. Augustine, where it grew profusely and was one of the earliest to bloom. The gossip columnist of the *Tatler* took note of the exceptionally early appearance of the flowers in January of 1901 that delighted northern visitors: "The appearance of yellow jasmine on the streets has been regarded as a harbinger of spring. The beautiful yellow flowers among the glistening green leaves is indeed a revelation to visitors who a day before were amid ice and snow."[48] The individual blossoms of the plant were even more transient than the short-lived magnolias and Cherokee roses, a quality that provides the theme for a sentimental verse in the *St. Augustine News:*

> You are so sweet, so bright and fair;
> Would you could stay with us always,
> To lend your glory everywhere.
> You live a day, then pass away
> Our common lot, alas! To share. . . .[49]

The theme of the poem was a common trope in the literature of flowers, and the sentiment would have been very familiar to the northern tourists who purchased Heade's flower paintings. The precision of Heade's craft gave his renditions a particular clarity and factuality, fixing lastingly in paint what remained impermanent in life. In northern parlors, Heade's paintings became enduring souvenirs of the short-lived pleasures of their owners' brief respite in "the land of flowers" and served as a regular antidote to the bare and flowerless vistas glimpsed outside their winter windows.

Martin Johnson Heade in Florida

CHAPTER FOUR

Poet of Wetlands / Prophet of Conservation

S EVERAL FEATURES MAKE *On the San Sebastian River, Florida* (plate 14) exceptional among Heade's representations of the Florida landscape. Despite the prevalence of spectacular tropical storms in the coastal region, this is one of only two known Florida scenes that reverted to the drama of rapidly changing weather portrayed in works such as *Thunder Storm on Narragansett Bay* (fig. 11, p. 19). *On the San Sebastian* is more specific than any other Heade view of Florida in its reference to human presence: two boats have clearly visible occupants, and various buildings can be detected scattered behind and among the trees along the distant horizon. Two towers and a pair of smokestacks, one emitting a thin trail of white smoke, identify the distant vista precisely: these are distinguishing features of the Hotel Ponce de Leon. This is almost certainly the painting described shortly after the opening of the hotel as one of the most outstanding in Heade's studio, "a beautiful landscape scene of the San Sebastian marshes,

with a view of the city of St. Augustine, and the towers . . . in the distance."[1] Heade, who had moved into his studio at the hotel even before the official opening of the complex, probably deliberately intended to draw attention to this dramatic new feature of the St. Augustine skyline.

The specificity of the image makes it possible to locate the painter's viewpoint with some precision. St. Augustine historian David Nolan has pointed out that the artist was working from "a favorite scenic overlook for artists here during the Flagler era," and one can still observe the same general view from the bridge that crosses the San Sebastian River on State Road 16.[2] Felix de Crano, Heade's neighbor in the Ponce de Leon studios, painted a closer view of the same group of buildings in a small watercolor now in the Lightner Museum, St. Augustine (fig. 50). Neither painting is dated, but since Heade shows the power plant functioning, his picture must have been completed close to the opening of the hotel in January 1888. The dome immediately to the right in De Crano's view of the skyline, and still clearly visible to a modern spectator looking from the State Road 16 Bridge, is missing from Heade's painting. This dome identifies the Memorial Presbyterian Church, dedicated in March 1890, in honor of Henry Flagler's daughter Jennie Louise, who had died exactly one year before. The Venetian Renaissance style building was and is regarded as one of the "chief adornments of the city," and its dome "contributed to the dignity and grace of St. Augustine's picturesque skyline."[3] Since it is unthinkable that Heade would omit such a prominent feature from his picture, he must have completed the work before the church was built, reinforcing the probability that this was the painting described in 1888.

"Heade painted the towers of Flagler's hotel and its power plant," as has been perceptively suggested, "both as a tribute to his patron and an acknowledgement of industry's inevitable encroachment on his beloved marshland."[4] Stebbins sees an analogy between the smoking power plant in *On the San Sebastian* and the passing train and railroad trestle in *Lynn Meadows* (Yale University Art Gallery), 1863, an early view of tidal mudflats in Massachusetts. Both smokestack and train may be manifestations of what Leo Marx, in a classic study, dubbed "the machine in the garden," evidence of the invasive presence of modern technology in the previously unsullied American Eden.[5] Not only did the Ponce de

Leon require elaborate technological support, including electric generators and complex hydraulics, but its construction also necessitated a remaking of the landscape. The orange grove that became the site of the hotel stood on marshy ground around Maria Sanchez Creek. Concerned about the unhealthy associations of such land with malaria outbreaks, Flagler instructed his builders to efface all evidence of the original tidal marsh. They accomplished this by filling both creek and low-lying land with tons of sand.[6]

Fig. 50. Felix de Crano. *Skyline, St. Augustine.* After 1890. Watercolor on paper. 14¼ × 24½ in. Lightner Museum Collection, St. Augustine, Florida.

Perhaps even as Heade portrayed the beauty of the tidal marshes along the San Sebastian, he meant to acknowledge the potential threat to such environments posed by the rapid expansion of the city. In 1887, when the full hustle and bustle of Flagler's remaking of the ancient city was under way, a visitor from Macon, Georgia, encountered a sight quite similar to that shown in *On the San Sebastian* as he approached St. Augustine from the north. He admired his first view of the city, "gazing out over a salt marsh with the St. Sebastian River twisted about it like a great silver band washed up by the tide and held prisoner under the long fingers of the green grass," but left the city regretfully bemoaning the invasion of modern buildings and noisy tourists.[7] Heade was an active participant in and beneficiary of the development activities that were going on apace in St. Augustine and that threatened to impinge steadily on the surrounding waterways and marshes as well, but the somber and ambiguous tone of this painting suggests that he was also troubled by these incursions into the still relatively unspoiled natural environment.

The San Sebastian River and its marshes had evidently been one of the first landscape subjects undertaken by Heade after he settled in St. Augustine. Julia Mary Weeks de Forest, a visitor from New York City, encountered Heade while taking a carriage ride along the San Sebastian in 1884. Recalling the meeting in her diary, she noted that this was a favorite painting spot for the artist and that he had already done a number of pictures of the river and its marshes.[8] From his cottage on the other side of the peninsula that is formed between the San Sebastian and the Matanzas rivers, Heade had another prospect of marshes. He had urged his friend Eben Loomis to send his daughter (Mabel Loomis Todd, whom Heade had befriended and advised about her painting) to "come down and paint some of her pictures in my studio by the edge of the salt meadow."[9] It is not always clear which of Heade's Florida landscapes represented the marshes of the Matanzas and San Sebastian estuary, but several insistently horizontal views, including *Florida Marsh with a Tree* (fig. 51), seem likely candidates.

Heade's paintings of northern coastal marshes were really pastoral scenes, showing the routine agricultural use of the areas, from which the rich salt grasses were regularly harvested and piled into the characteristic haycocks that punctuate Heade's images. In contrast, *Florida Marsh with a Tree* shows a wide-open vista with few alleviating details. The bareness, approaching barrenness, of this intensely horizontal composition contrasts with the relatively busy northern marsh pictures. In a positive sense it may "reflect the freer air of Heade's Florida, not yet clogged by too many people and too much civilization."[10] *On the San Sebastian*, probably painted a bit later than this empty view, hinted that the southern wetland, like its northern counterparts, would soon show more and more marks of human intrusion. The boatmen who facilitate the viewer's mental progress into the landscape are reminiscent of the two boatmen in Heade's early *Lake George* (fig. 16, p. 27). In that work, the artist leaves the lake and surrounding mountains otherwise pristine, belying the considerable human intervention that would have actually been visible in this popular resort. The picture of the Hotel Ponce de Leon viewed across the San Sebastian and its marshes engaged in no such dissimilation and may offer a portent of changes that will ultimately affect the landscape more widely.

Nancy Frazier has argued that the pastoral vision of salt-marsh agriculture portrayed in Heade's northern marshes represented a way of life that was beginning to disappear at precisely the time that the artist began to portray it: "[B]y the end of the Civil War, estuaries were the focal points for industrial growth. That, combined with exhaustion of its nutrients and abandonment of the farms, brought the 200-year-long development of salt marsh agriculture screeching not just to a halt, but into reverse."[11] She interprets the stormy skies depicted in so many of these works as ominous indicators of the troubled status of the marshlands.[12] Florida, especially the coastal areas, offers a range of changeable skies and pyrotechnic storms that one would expect to be irresistible to the artist who had painted the inky skies and haunting light effects of *Thunder Storm on Narragansett Bay* (fig. 11, p. 19). Indeed, *On the San Sebastian River, Florida* provides one of the artist's last great renderings of such extreme coastal weather: sky, land, and water merge into an impenetrable gloom on the left; to the right, a still slightly sickly light breaks forth and shoots along the horizon line; in the center of the sky, light and dark clash in an explosion of fluorescent pink cloud, and an only slightly less lurid pink spreads like a stain over the surface of the water below. Clearly, Heade reveled

Fig. 51. Martin Johnson Heade. *Florida Marsh with a Tree.* c. 1883–90. Oil on canvas. 13 × 25 ⁵/₁₆ in. Private collection. Photograph courtesy of Vose Galleries of Boston.

in these effects for their own sake, but it is hard to resist the idea that here some sort of omen may be intended, especially since none of Heade's other Florida paintings show such intensely dramatic weather. If these other views, whether of salt marshes, swampy riverbanks, or inland cypress bogs, are also meant to strike a warning about the fragility and potential destruction of wetlands, they convey their message in hushed tones, through the very transient qualities of the light effects they preserve. Although a few works, including *The Great Florida Marsh* (plate 4) and *Florida River Scene* (plate 8), contrast rain clouds with breaking sunshine, the Florida landscapes more commonly show the fading tints of sunrise or sunset or the last glow of amber- or green-tinged twilight.

Heade's sympathy for swamps and marshes was certainly unusual during a period when most of the associations of such lands were with muck and mosquitoes, but, as I have already pointed out, his experience in hunting and fishing had taught him that this half-land, half-water was also a prodigiously fertile breeding ground for all sorts of wildlife. At a time when most people thought of wetlands as places to be ditched and drained and reformed, so that they could be made productive for settlement or agriculture, Heade had enough foresight to discern both an innate beauty and an innate value in such lands. His pleas for the protection and preservation of the wetlands environment and its denizens are primarily

found in two places: in his many essays and letters to *Forest and Stream* and, most eloquently, in the moving poetry of his wetlands paintings.

As was customary for *Forest and Stream* contributors, Heade selected a pseudonym to identify his writings. He had used the nickname "Didymus" on much of his public writing, including poetry, as early as 1845, and it probably was meant to express an affinity to St. Thomas, the apostle whose surname, "Didymus," meant "The Twin."[13] Thomas was best known as the "doubting disciple," and so it has been assumed that the name was meant to indicate Heade's inherent skepticism, a quality borne out in his *Forest and Stream* notes, where he often chided his fellow contributors for the sin of "Münchhausenism," a term he coined from the name of the notorious eighteenth-century German purveyor of tall tales, Baron von Münchhausen. Many of his short notes were directed at correcting the exaggerations or fabrications he believed that he had detected in the observations of other amateur naturalists; others were contributions to ongoing discussions about subjects such as game preserves or market hunting. He also regularly wrote short observation-based comments on various species, especially birds, and much longer essays on his favorite topics, including hummingbirds.

By the standards of his time, Heade was a careful, appropriately skeptical, amateur naturalist whose conclusions were based on long and patient empirical observations. The obituary published in *Forest and Stream* called him "an intelligent and sympathetic student of natural history."[14] His notes featured charming anecdotes of the hours spent sitting with his wife on their piazza, enticing tiny hummingbirds to feed from hand-held vials of sugar water and observing their habits. In our own time, a hunting and fishing magazine seems poles apart from a scientific journal. At the end of the nineteenth century, however, the observations that writers like Heade published in *Forest and Stream* were considered both valid and valued contributions to the field biology of the day. Perhaps even more surprising to modern sensibilities, "there seldom was much of a dividing line between ornithologists and sportsmen."[15]

It is important that Heade's wider comments on conservation also be understood within the context of his times, because they might otherwise appear contradictory and disconcerting to modern readers whose environmentalism is often associated with animal rights concerns. Heade's love of the natural world, and his particular affinity for wetlands environments, was clearly a direct product of his lifetime love of fishing and hunting. Today's readers are often made uncomfortable by the idea that someone like Heade could enjoy killing sports and even be brought closer to nature through them, and the result is sometimes a rather wrong-headed attempt to reconcile the perceived psychological contradictions, as in the writing of David Miller:

> Heade's love of hunting and his preoccupation with stricter game laws (particularly in his later years) reveal an attitude of ritual antagonism to nature; his numerous articles in *Forest and Stream*, written in the 1880s and 1890s, attest to this. The artist commonly indulged in unrepentant accounts of his killing sprees. . . . Yet, paradoxically, Heade also complained about the wanton shooting of animals. . . . It appears that Heade was deeply concerned with enacting a rigorous code of sportsmanship, a patterned response to nature, in order to achieve control in the absence of prophetic vision.[16]

In fact, Heade's writings, alternating nostalgic reminiscences about long-ago hunts and the abundant shooting opportunities of the past with calls for tighter game controls and new conservation measures, are completely in keeping with the general tenor of *Forest and Stream*, the most influential of several new national periodicals devoted to sport hunting. These popular journals recognized that decimation of wetlands and indiscriminate hunting would mark the end of their favorite pastime, and they took an important leadership role in promoting the first efforts at wetlands preservation. Sportsmen, whose interaction with the natural landscape was active rather than passive, had first learned to appreciate the topography of the inland swamps and coastal marshes that proponents of picturesque landscape had dismissed as ugly. For the hunters and fishermen who spent long hours immersed in this landscape, "so-called wastelands were frequently the repositories of fond memories and keen anticipations," and they were leaders in recognizing the subtle beauties of the wetlands as well as their vital role in the game supply.[17]

The increased activism fostered by these sporting publications set the tone for a gradual aesthetic reevaluation of wetlands landscape in which literature, landscape architecture, and painting all played a role. When the famous landscape architect Frederick Law Olmsted created an unprecedented "wetlands park" in the Back Bay area of Boston, his procedures, described by Ann Vileisis, were remarkably close to the compositional principles of Heade: "Olmsted wrote about creating his salt marsh landscape as Martin J. Heade might have written about composing a salt marsh painting. He described adding 'slashes of golden rods and asters' to the cordgrass just as the painter might describe adding brush strokes of color here and there. Though his palette of vegetation was informed by biology, Olmsted's choices were largely aesthetic."[18]

Just as Heade continued to hark back to early experiences by interspersing paintings of the northeastern salt marsh and Brazilian hummingbirds with his views of Florida, his articles for *Forest and Stream* regularly alternated reminiscences of his boyhood and his wide-ranging midlife rambles with observations about present-day conditions in Florida. Inevitably, these recollections are tinged with a sense of loss, not only bemoaning, in typical *Forest and Stream* fashion, the disappearance of the abundant game from the landscape, but also chronicling the devastation of the land itself. A nostalgic account of boyhood exploits in Pennsylvania concludes with a peroration on the destruction of the natural beauty of the Delaware River: "I have been on the Juniata and other lovely streams, but I have never seen a more beautiful river than the Delaware before the march of civilization with its railroads and canals took every vestige of its beauty away forever."[19] Although the tropical scenery of Florida rivers was dramatically different from the Delaware of Heade's youth, the fact that the state had not yet suffered the "civilizing" influences that had destroyed the Pennsylvania riverbanks must have increased its appeal to the artist at the same time that his past experience made him all-too-aware of its possible future fate.

From his first visit, Heade clearly perceived the ready connections between his favorite northern scenes of salt marshes and the various wetlands of Florida. *Evening, Lake Alto, Florida* (plate 3), 1883, is probably his first Florida landscape. It depicts the marshy inland area near Waldo, where Heade spent two pleasant weeks during his exploratory visit to Florida. This canvas is exactly the same size as the northern view called *Sunset Marshes: Bringing in the Hay*, 1883 (private collection, Philadelphia), and possibly the two works were intended as pendants, especially since both are signed and dated in the same way.[20] The distribution of patches of water, clumps of trees, and fluffy cumulus clouds is similar in the two works, and the horizons are placed nearly identically. The Florida work substitutes a diagonally projecting bare branch and scattered cows for the haystacks, hay carts, and harvesters that mark the progression into space in the northern picture. Both paintings show Heade's characteristic attention to the ever-changing nuance of light. His representation of the dying evening light at Lake Alto is particularly effective: an evanescent mist of pink barely brushes the clouds near the horizon, and a momentary glow whitens the edges of the clouds, turns the reeds iridescent, imparts a mirror-sheen to the pools of water, and even gives the single white cow a startling, ghostly presence. It seems almost as if the artist was testing the properties of the Florida subject to see if it could serve his aesthetic as well as the northern marshes had.

The felicitous parallelism of northern and southern wetlands is the subject of a pair of paintings that, judging from their style, must have been painted very late in Heade's life. The two small canvases, *Florida Marsh: Dawn* (fig. 52) and *Northern Marsh: Sunset* (fig. 53) were purchased by Flagler and presented as a gift to his friend George Sidney Prindle. Although they set up a contrast between North and South by emphasizing either haystacks or palm trees, and introduce the classic opposition of morning and evening, the affinities of these two wetland vistas are emphasized much more strongly than their disparities. These two landscapes seem less directly linked to specific sites than earlier Heade marshlands. Their loose execution, understated tonalities, and intimate scale enhance the sense that these are memory images, perhaps laments as much as celebrations.

The newly recognized scenic qualities of marshy lands, so vividly conveyed in Heade's canvases, did not reveal the incredible diversity of species sheltered by the wetlands or the integral part played by these creatures in the food chains upon which both land and sea depend. It was easiest and most obvious to see the importance of wetlands to "the most visual and charismatic residents of the ecosystem," the many types of birds who "breathed life and animation into the natural world."[21] The concerns of the amateur naturalists and bird-lovers and those of the hunters came together in the pages of *Forest and Stream*, and Martin Johnson Heade was not the only one to address those seemingly contradictory interests.

Forest and Stream began with the declared program of promoting properly enforced game laws and other measures that would ensure conservation of game and gradually began to take on other causes as well, but the battle was clearly an uphill one. In 1883, ten years after the creation of the magazine, "Didymus" declared the

Fig. 52. Martin Johnson Heade. *Florida Marsh: Dawn*. c. 1895–1904. Oil on canvas. 8¼ × 16 in.
Maryann K. and Alvin Friedman, Washington, D.C.

Fig. 53. Martin Johnson Heade. *Northern Marsh: Sunset.* c. 1895–1904. Oil on canvas. 8¼ × 16 in.
Maryann K. and Alvin Friedman, Washington, D.C.

first decade's efforts to have been wasted: "Sportsmen expected to shoot cartloads of game from their parlors in every part of the country," he declared hyperbolically, "but instead of our expectations being realized, the only progress made in sporting matters has been backward!" He went on to assert, "a sportsman can scarcely find a snipe or mud-hen without going to St. Augustine," and, indeed that is exactly what the author had made up his own mind to do when he penned the article.[22]

Unfortunately, by the time Heade settled in Florida, the decimation of its avian population was already well under way. The depredations wrought by increasing floods of indiscriminate and unregulated recreational hunters were multiplied geometrically by the wholesale slaughter perpetrated by market hunters who lived by selling game, especially the plume hunters set on supplying the latest in millinery fashions. Heade had written a report to *Forest and Stream* on his hunting experiences during his initial exploratory trip to Florida and had severely criticized St. Augustine's policy of forbidding shooting in the marshes immediately surrounding the city. The editors pointed out that the revival of the bird population around the city was only the result of the strict enforcement of this rule, enacted in an attempt to reverse "the extermination of birds . . . that took place in the vicinity of St. Augustine when the rush of Northern visitors first set in there. The gunners spared nothing that had wings."[23]

Throughout his years in Florida, Heade continued to reminisce about the abundant wildlife and the memorable hunting excursions of his youth, and many of those accounts may reek of bloodthirsty excess to a modern reader. Increasingly, however, his articles shift toward emphasis on conservation, calling for enforcement of strict hunting seasons and for bag limits, and joining other *Forest and Stream* authors in roundly condemning market hunting, plume hunting, and the killing of songbirds. In 1886, George Bird Grinnell, editor of *Forest and Stream*, created the first Audubon Society, calling for all those interested in the plight of bird populations to sign pledges to assist in protecting the species. This was the heart of his proposal: "We propose the formation of an association for the protection of wild birds and their eggs, which should be called the Audubon society. Its membership is to be free to every one who is willing to lend a helping hand in forwarding the objects for which it is formed. These objects shall be to prevent, so far as possible, (1) the killing of any wild birds not used for food, (2) the destruction of nests or eggs of any wild bird, and (3) the wearing of feathers as ornaments or trimming for dress."[24]

By 1888 the response to Grinnell's initial plea was so overwhelming that the magazine could no longer administer the membership and the group was disbanded, but soon Audubon societies were being formed all over the country.[25] There is a long hiatus in Heade's contributions to *Forest and Stream* about this time (1883–91), but when his regular entries resume in the 1890s more and more of them are directed to conservation issues.

In 1884, Heade confessed to his friend Eben Loomis that he had been guilty of shooting a Great Blue Heron on the Sabbath, because his wife had wanted the wings.[26] Presumably Mrs. Heade wished to use these wings to decorate a hat in the typically outrageous fashion of the day, a practice responsible for some of the most egregious wildlife slaughter: "The style of adorning women's hats and clothing with feathers and wings had become so prevalent in the latter portion of the century that in many places it was more common to see feathers on hats than on wild birds. During a stroll through Manhattan in 1886, one ornithologist counted 542 birds—all stuffed and mounted whole atop women's gaudy hats."[27] By 1892 when, as "Didymus," he praised and promoted the efforts of the nascent Audubon Society to boycott the wearing of birds and bird parts in ladies' bonnets, Heade must have forgotten or been thoroughly ashamed of his own earlier transgression on behalf of millinery excess. The destructive practices of plume hunters were now denounced as a "bloody business": "In Florida, where I eat my daily bread, the slaughter has been frightful. I have heard of men, who claim to be sportsmen, tell of shooting into a tree where egrets collect by the hundreds to roost, and then in the morning picking up those that have attractive plumage and leaving the rest to rot. Now, I believe when such fellows die, their souls, if they have any, will be kept in a state of miserable unrest for several eternities by the screams and flutterings of birds that they have slain in wanton barbarity."[28]

The herons and egrets that supply regular grace notes in Heade's paintings of Florida landscape (plates 1, 4, 5; see fig. 51) take on an almost elegiac quality considering fears for the survival of these species. In his writings, Heade regularly returned to the subject, calling on both fashion-conscious women and state legislators to put an end to the "devilish business" that results in such wanton and wasteful acts as "shooting out a roost," destroying mature birds, and leaving their young to starve.[29] "Only a few years ago one of the great attractions of Florida was the myriads of beautiful plumaged birds throughout the State," wrote Heade in 1894, "and now, on account of legislative stupidity, they are on the ragged edge of extermination, and half the charm of Florida is gone."[30]

Heade's fears about species destruction may also have added a poignant note to the hummingbird and orchid pictures he continued to paint regularly in Florida (plates 10, 15). Stuffed hummingbirds regularly appeared as hat decorations, and, once again, Heade called for "the tender-hearted ladies" to bring market pressure to bear by rejecting this fashion for avian ornaments. He increased the sentimental pressure of his appeal by reminding his readers that the "millions upon millions of lovely little creatures" killed for their skins in Brazil were invariably harvested during breeding season when their plumage was brightest, "and when the old birds are killed the young ones must, of course, die a miserable death by starvation."[31] The regular reports of Heade's new work and studio contents in the *Tatler* demonstrated that his output of hummingbird pictures continued steadily into his final years. Stebbins has pointed out that in the latest of these works (plate 15) "the orchid plants themselves became old and unhealthy for the first time," and suggests that the torn, chewed, and mottled leaves of these plants might reflect Heade's own growing intimations of mortality.[32] The emblematic connotations of the damaged and dying plants could just as easily be intended as a comment on the imperiled status of the South American hummingbirds.

"Didymus" enlarged the scope of his calls for conservation throughout the 1890s, inveighing bitterly against the butchery of "game hogs" and against the blindness of lawmakers who failed to pass and enforce appropriate legislation to stem the tide of destruction. Market hunters of any stripe, whom he regarded as too lazy to do real work, and game hunters who engaged in wholesale slaughter for its own sake were among his particular targets. He also deplored the practice (promoted in hotels and private game preserves) of shooting or fishing for record catches, resulting in exorbitant kills. He reacted in horror to hunters' tales of cruel practices ranging from smoking out opossums to wantonly picking off alligators from the decks of steamboats. Nor did "Didymus" merely

rant aimlessly about the folly of his fellow humans in thus laying waste to nature and her creatures. He made practical suggestions ranging from specific legislation to enact taxes and licensing fees, to better enforcement of existing game laws, to the embargo against plumes and other ornithological hat ornaments that he proposed to the ladies. A horrified review of a book by one George O. Shields (who published in *Forest and Stream* under the pen name "Coquina") describes the "Exterminatory Peregrinations" indulged in by that "game butcher" as he rampaged up the St. Johns River and down the Gulf coast, leaving a trail of wounded and slaughtered alligators, dying plume birds, and various other maimed and moribund fish, birds, and mammals in his wake. Such cruel and indiscriminate practices, said Heade, demonstrated the need for specific new legislation including a nonresident tax and a coupon system to restrict the amount of game killed by any individual. Such legislation, Heade felt, might make a start on compensating for some of the depredations of the past: "the horse is stolen. All we can do now, however is to make the best of it, and trust that with a better administration of our native resources the waste places may once more be made vocal with songs of birds, the wilderness may be brightened with the brilliant colors of our native plume birds, and even the ugly and unamiable alligator may greet the eye of the traveler on our fresh-water lakes."[33]

"Didymus" was not always so sanguine about the possibilities that legislation could or would succeed in abating the destruction of Florida's natural riches. He briefly takes on two causes that are still very much in the forefront of Florida environmental concerns: the sea turtle and the manatee. From the pessimism of his tones in considering the prospects for these two species, he would probably be surprised to learn that any of them have survived into the twenty-first century. He is scathing in renouncing the failure of the legislators to outlaw the harvesting of turtle eggs and even harsher in his sarcastic prediction of the future of the manatee: "Florida has legislators of wonderful foresight, who can always be relied on to see the danger of exterminating game and plumage birds after they have disappeared, and it's hardly worth while to trouble ourselves about the rapidly disappearing manatee, for our wise solons will attend to that, as they attend to everything else in that line."[34]

Heade's *Forest and Stream* writings on behalf of endangered species are not matched by written proposals for the environments they occupy; his pleading on behalf of the wetlands is confined to the far greater eloquence of his paintings. Few of his Florida landscapes are dated, but Stebbins believes that both the quantity and quality of the landscapes began to fall off toward the end of the 1890s, and he sees a weakening of Heade's powers in works such as *Florida Sunset with Two Cows* (Alexander Gallery, New York), which show very generalized details and "perfunctory" paint handling.[35] The increasingly ethereal and nonspecific qualities of

Heade's late landscapes can also be considered symptomatic of the elegiac mode of the works. Early Florida output, including the first pictures of the St. Johns River and the large-scale paintings commissioned by Flagler, celebrated the characteristic beauties of the state and self-consciously introduced this new terrain to both tourists and a national audience. The two small sunset views in the Parrish Art Museum (figs. 54, 55) no longer show those qualities of close, patient, even scientific observation that were so striking in Heade's first views of Florida. Instead, a few shimmering and insubstantial elements are suspended in a dreamy vapor of green, pink, and violet tones, emphasizing the innate fragility of the land. In all probability these works were based on recollection and imagination, rather than on nature, and their ephemeral qualities suggest the fleeting shades of memory.

Heade seems to have remained quite fit and healthy well into his later years. Church writes enviously about his continued good health and wonders at the reports that Heade and his wife are taking avidly to bicycling when Church himself, younger by six years, was so crippled by "rheumatic infirmities" that he was unable to walk any distance unaided.[36] A photograph from the 1890s shows Heade with his bicycle (fig. 56); another, not illustrated, shows the artist painting from nature while the bicycle rests nearby.[37] His activities must have been circumscribed after the turn of the century, however, and he increasingly concentrated on the floral pieces that

Fig. 54. Martin Johnson Heade. *Sunset: Florida Marsh*. c. 1895–1904. Oil on panel. 6⅛ × 12⅜ in.
The Parrish Art Museum, Southampton, New York. Clark Collection. 1958.4.12.

Fig. 55. Martin Johnson Heade. *Florida Sunset, with Palm Trees.* c. 1895–1904. Oil on academy board. 6⅛ × 12 in. The Parrish Art Museum, Southampton, New York. Littlejohn Collection. 1961.3.54.

Fig. 56. *Martin Johnson Heade and His Bicycle*. 1890s. Photograph.
Private collection.

could be completed indoors. As the winter season opened in 1902, the *Tatler* reported that Heade was ill and unable to preside at the receptions in his Ponce de Leon studio, but that a Mr. Swaim would do the honors for him.[38] The following year he was back in the Ponce de Leon studio, though the paper now described him as "one of the oldest living artists."[39] A visiting editor from *Forest and Stream* found him "tall and erect and clear of eye at eighty-three, active and strong, and ever ready for action."[40] By January of 1904, the aging artist had abandoned the Ponce de Leon in favor of his home studio at 105 San Marco Avenue, where, however, he was still "pleased to show his pictures and sketches to visitors."[41] In these final years the catalog of his studio contents is heavily weighted to the flower pictures.

In his Florida years, the artist who had once roved the world from Europe to South America and across the North American continent gradually narrowed his physical scope and may have become more and more housebound in his last months. Yet visitors found him mentally acute and able to paint such vivid pictures with both word and brush that any physical limitations did not confine him. The *Forest and Stream* editor does not complain that he missed out on a promised hunting trip because of "a slight local affliction soon mended" that kept "Didymus" from the woods, but recounts that instead he spent an afternoon with him "hunting and fishing in many lands." Heade's imaginative skills were still keen, and his

Martin Johnson Heade in Florida

present setting far from restrictive: "In the charming appointments of this home, the many windows where the sun can come in, the hanging of a drapery, the adjustment of pictures, the rugs harmonious, the prettily groomed lawn overlooking the water, presided over by Her who should rule all our destinies, I spent a delightful hour. The best hunting trip in my life was experienced in Didymus's library. . . . It was so real."[42]

Heade continued to paint and to pen articles for *Forest and Stream* until shortly before his death on September 4, 1904. The obituary published by *Forest and Stream* suggests that Florida had indeed proven to be a Fountain of Youth for Heade, keeping him alert and productive until his final days: "Nor did his skill diminish with the advance of age. The last year of life found him at the easel painting landscapes characterized by the same wonderful atmospheric effects that had won admiration for his earlier work, and fixing on the abiding canvas the evanescent floral beauties of a Florida springtime. A picture sweet in the memory of those who saw it was that of the artist in his St. Augustine home, painting northern marsh land and southern flower, and joying in the possession of faculties unimpaired and a hand which had not lost its cunning."[43]

The *Tatler* reprinted the *Forest and Stream* obituary in January, when the season reopened in St. Augustine. The paper went on to note that, "In the death of Martin Johnson Heade . . . St. Augustine lost one of her most distinguished citizens, a gentleman of irreproachable character and high attainments, who had traveled in strange and out of the way places."[44] Heade was buried in Evergreen Cemetery, Brooklyn, New York.[45] His wife and heir, Elizabeth Smith Heade, stayed on in St. Augustine, at least during the winter season, and kept the cottage until 1912.[46] Until 1908, the last year that the *Tatler* was published, we can read of her regular receptions for visitors (and prospective purchasers) in the old studio at the Ponce de Leon. The yearly accounts of her studio receptions speak of Heade's work in tones that increasingly acknowledge that these works are no longer fashionable:

> Mrs. Heade has placed a number of the late Martin Johnson Heade's paintings in Studio No. 1, Studio Row, and will be there most days after 10 o'clock to show them. Some of the paintings are for sale and are worth seeing. Mr. Heade belonged to the Raphael school. That has not been in vogue for the last 15 years, nevertheless his work is exceptionally good, and every detail of petal and leaf carefully painted. Years ago he painted landscapes that commanded high prices and are highly valued by their owners. More recently Mr. Heade painted flowers, roses, daisies, magnolias, yellow jasmines, and the Cherokee that are typical of Florida. He painted orchids as they grow in the wilds of Brazil, giving the flower a texture that cannot be imitated. Mrs. Heade will welcome visitors whether purchasers or not.[47]

Heade's fall from fashion had begun well before his death. Posthumous reports in the *Tatler* noted that his "absolute faithfulness to

Fig. 57. *Moving the Martin Johnson Heade House in Front of Castillo.* 1954. Photograph. From the Collection of the Museum of Arts and Sciences, Daytona Beach, Florida. Gift of Kenneth Worcester Dow and Mary Mohan Dow.

Fig. 58. *Moving the Martin Johnson Heade House in Front of Mission Shrine Sign.* 1954. Photograph. From the Collection of the Museum of Arts and Sciences, Daytona Beach, Florida. Gift of Kenneth Worcester Dow and Mary Mohan Dow.

nature and painstaking attention to detail" did not appeal to those who favored the "present broad style of painting," a manner tempered by French Impressionist influence. "Mr. Heade was greatly opposed to the latter day conceptions of art, never wavering in his ideas."[48] Despite the dazzling promise of its first years, the Hotel Ponce de Leon also declined rapidly in popularity, becoming only a brief stopping-off place for the fashionable guests who followed Flagler himself further south to Palm Beach. Even when Flagler

again made a point of spending part of the season in St. Augustine, as he did from 1905 until his death in 1913, the fortunes of the hotel never completely recovered, although it continued to operate as a resort for more than another half century. In 1967, the Hotel Ponce de Leon closed its doors after eighty seasons. Fortunately, however, the spectacular buildings were preserved and transformed into Flagler College, and today the old ateliers of Studio Row have become classrooms for a new generation of artists.[49]

Martin Johnson Heade in Florida

Heade's St. Augustine home did not fare so well as the hotel and its studios, despite a valiant attempt to preserve it. In 1954, the Roman Catholic Diocese bought the land where the house stood, planning to build a church there. This church now forms the entrance to the precinct including the Mission of Nombre de Dios, Our Lady of La Leche Shrine, and a large cross marking the site where the first mass in St. Augustine was supposed to have been celebrated. However, local art collector Kenneth Worcester Dow was determined to save the artist's house, which he purchased and moved temporarily to a nearby lot (figs. 57, 58). A short time later, the temporary site fell victim to the Florida Department of Transportation, which decided to widen the road. Unable to find an alternative location for the Heade house, Dow allowed its demolition.[50]

Martin Johnson Heade's flourishing late career in Florida seemed a perfect fulfillment of the advertising claims that once sought to lure tourists and retirees to a new Eden where they might imbibe the influences of Ponce de León's legendary Fountain of Youth. Indeed, his paintings played a part in creating and sustaining those claims. Despite his advancing years, Heade's Florida period was vital and thoroughly original and produced an artistic statement of prophetic force. He cataloged the unique beauties of the new state, proffering an earthly paradise filled with splendors of utmost subtlety. His sense of the innate fragility of these new yet vulnerable lands was informed by his past experiences, and he offered a powerful message of conservation for the future, a message that needs to be heard more urgently than ever at the beginning of the twenty-first century.

Text for Color Plates

Plate 1: *The St. Johns River*, c. 1890s

A year before Martin Johnson Heade arrived in Florida, George M. Barbour reported in his handbook of the state, "Nearly all tourists in Florida 'do the St. John's.'" He gave this description of the varied environments to be found along the journey: "The lower St. John's presents an attractive *Southern* scene; the middle St. John's presents a semi-tropical scene of jungles and orange-groves; but the upper St. John's is the truly tropical region, deeply impressive, more easily remembered than described." It appears to be this upper region that Heade depicted in this painting, perhaps the region above Lake Monroe where the river itself is "little more than a narrow and very crooked creek" and a deceptive mixture of land and water spreads out in every direction:

> It is a flat, level region of savannas, much resembling the vast prairies of Illinois. In all directions the eye ranges to the horizon, with nothing to break the monotony. But though monotonous, it is not uninteresting. These savannas, or prairies, are everywhere densely covered with luxuriant growths of marshy grasses and maiden-cane . . . with occasional clumps of timber, consisting sometimes of but three or four trees, and sometimes being several acres in extent. The trees are nearly or quite all of palmetto, and lend a distinctly tropical appearance to the scenery. They much resemble small islands dotted over the surface of a great lake.
>
> Throughout this entire region were to be seen hundreds of cattle grazing on the rich vegetation, which is said to be greatly liked by them, and very fattening.[1]

Plate 2: *Haystacks*, c. 1876–82

Martin Johnson Heade may have brought this painting with him when he moved to Florida, where it was acquired by his patron, Henry Morrison Flagler, who probably also owned *The Great Swamp* (fig. 18, p. 31). He continued to produce new variations on the expansive and ever-changing view of earth, water, and sky in the northeastern salt marsh. His discovery of poetry and spiritual force in a previously neglected terrain that lacked the conventional markers of the picturesque was ahead of its time. By 1916 traditionally sublime subjects had been so belabored in both literature and art that the "life seems to have been painted or written out of them." Richard Le Galliene declared that mountains and cataracts had become so banal that they had "come to seem like Nature's stage properties." The marsh, however, promised endless opportunities for poetic or painterly representation:

> Whatever it may lack for some eyes—and its beauty is by no means for all—it has one advantage over the profiles and permanently featured landscape, the characteristic of perpetual change. It can never grow hackneyed, for it is never twice the same. . . . Its whole life is in its subtly modulated expressiveness. With each incoming and outgoing tide, it is a new creation of pure effect, a picture that is a musical composition made visible, from moment to moment growing through unforeseen rhythms and tones, at the will and accident of water and light and wind and cloud. . . . Wilderness, horizon, and water. The salt-marsh, as nothing else in nature, brings these together in a satisfying unity.[2]

Plate 3: *Evening, Lake Alto, Florida,* 1883

This is believed to be Martin Johnson Heade's first Florida landscape. Lake Alto is situated near Waldo, where Heade spent two pleasant weeks during his first exploratory trip to the state. He was investigat-

ing the promise of spectacular hunting and fishing advertised by the hotels of the state and had generally been rather disappointed in both the shooting and the accommodations. His side trip to Waldo apparently came about almost by accident but proved most enjoyable: "As I was strongly disposed to indulge my youthful passion for shooting, I interviewed every acquaintance who had been to Florida, and came to the conclusion that for good quail shooting I must leave the St. John's River; so I left for Ocala, but got left at Waldo, and finding friends and a very well-kept house, I concluded to hang up my hat and send for my baggage—especially as they reported shooting and fishing unsurpassed. I passed two weeks there, and did not regret it, though the shooting and fishing proved a fiction."[3]

Heade reported that Waldo was "about the only place in the state where one can live comfortably at a reasonable price," in contrast to Ocala, where he found the hotel "abominable." Of Waldo, he concluded: "It's a healthy place but not very attractive, but it's a nice place for people who come for health and can't afford the prices on the St. Johns."[4] This landscape of Lake Alto is unique in showing the marshy inland prairie of Florida. Heade's later Florida landscapes stay closer to the standard tourist route along the St. Johns and the areas immediately around St. Augustine.

Plate 4: *The Great Florida Marsh,* 1886

The Great Florida Marsh was the first painting that Henry Morrison Flagler bought from Martin Johnson Heade, the beginning of a long and fruitful relationship between patron and artist. The painting celebrates the freshwater marshes of Florida, opening up new territory for the artist, who had already recognized the pictorial possibilities of the salt marshes of the northeastern United States. Heade was unusual, but not unique, in recognizing the beauty and fecundity of these wetlands. His fellow immigrant from the northeast, Harriet Beecher Stowe, had already realized that the swampy lands along the St. Johns River were filled with surprising charm and promise, as when she describes this patch of wetland near her home in Mandarin:

> This swamp is one of those crooks in our lot which occasions a never-ceasing conflict of spirit. It is a glorious, bewildering impropriety. The trees and shrubs in it grow as if they were possessed; and there is scarcely a month of the year that it does not flame forth in new blossoms. It is a perpetual flower-garden, where creepers run and tangle; where Nature has raptures and frenzies of growth, and conducts herself like a crazy drunken but beautiful *bacchante*. But what to do with it is not clear. The river rises and falls in it; and under all that tangle of foliage lies a foul sink of the blackest mud. The black, unsavory moccasin-snakes are said and believed to have their lair in those jungles, where foot of man cares not to tread. Gigantic bulrushes grow up; clumps of high water-grasses, willows, elms, maples, cypresses, Magnolia glauca (sweet-bay), make brave show of foliage. Below, the blue pickerel-weed, the St. John's lily, the blue iris, wild-roses, blossoming tufts of elder, together with strange flowers of names unspoken, make a goodly fellowship. The birds herd there in droves; red-birds glance like gems through the boughs; cat-birds and sparrows and jays babble and jargon there in the green labyrinths made by the tangling vines. We muse over it, mean-while enjoying the visible coming-on of spring in its foliage. The maples have great red leaves, curling with their own rapid growth; the elms feather out into graceful plumes; and the cypresses, as we said before, most brilliant of all spring greens, puts forth its fairy foliage. Verily it is the most gorgeous of improprieties, this swamp; and we will let it alone this year also, and see what will come of it. There are suggestions of ditching and draining, and what not, that shall convert the wild *bacchante* into a steady, orderly member of society. We shall see.[5]

Plate 5: *Tropical Sunset: Florida Marsh Scene with Cattle*, c.1885–90

This is one of many more intimate variations of the subject of *The Great Florida Sunset*, commissioned by Henry Flagler to adorn the new Hotel Ponce de Leon. Here the artist zooms in closer on the grazing cattle dimly visible in the distance in the bigger picture. Heade chose the moments just before and just after sunset for the majority of his Florida landscapes, with an occasional sunrise or passing rainstorm for variety. Unlike his friend and mentor Frederic E. Church, whose sunset views often approached stridency in their bold and jangling colors, Heade always chose more understated effects. Here the sun has already slipped beneath the horizon, and the brilliant colors of sunset are fading into darkness. The nearly imperceptible blending of day and night complements the marshy terrain, where land and water likewise merge without clear boundaries.

When Flagler opened his Palm Beach mansion, Whitehall, he had *The Great Florida Sunset* sent there so that he could continue to admire its subtle effects. He evidently took great pleasure in admiring similar effects in nature. Edwin Lefèvre sat watching the sunset over Lake Worth with an octogenarian Flagler as he concluded an interview in which he had tried to get Flagler to explain his reasons for undertaking his Florida endeavors:

> . . . I turned to this old, old man who had done so much and had talked so little; and . . . I asked him, I fear impatiently:
>
> "Doesn't this sky get into your soul? Doesn't this glow light it? Don't you love that water, that line of trees, that sky? Isn't this the real reason you do things here?"
>
> He turned to me, hesitated; then, very slowly, very quietly, he said: "Sometimes, at the close of day, when I am fortunate enough to be alone, I come here. . . . I look at the water and at the trees yonder and at the sunset." He turned to me and placed his hand on my shoulder. Then, earnestly, almost wistfully: "I often wonder if there is anything in the other world so beautiful as this."[6]

Plate 6: *View from Fern-Tree Walk, Jamaica*, 1887

Heade based this large painting, created specifically for Flagler's new Hotel Ponce de Leon, on his memories and sketches of Jamaica, which he visited in 1870. A late-nineteenth-century guidebook gives this description of Fern Gully, which appears to have been the inspiration for the site: "The scenery through this ravine is unique, and can be surpassed by few other places in the world. It is from forty to fifty feet in width, just wide enough for a good road; the sides rise perpendicular to the height of hundreds of feet; only the noonday sun penetrates to the road. The steep rocks on each side are literally covered with the loveliest of ferns, which grow in the richest profusion. Tree-ferns of magnificent proportions, as well as the tiniest and most delicate specimens, are seen. The forest trees, too, are laden with orchids and long creepers, which descend from the branches thirty feet or more to the surface below."[7]

Obviously Heade does not show exactly the narrow gorge described by travel books. Instead he opens up his vista to provide a spectacular view of the harbor to the right and to illuminate the many precisely rendered tropical specimens that are assembled to the left.[8] The exotic and varied plants would have complemented the botanical riches that flourished in the grounds and courtyards of Flagler's hotel complex.

Plate 7: *Florida Sunrise*, c. 1887–1900

The small sailing boats that seem to skim along the surface of the glassy water are curiously dwarfed by the enormous width of the St. Johns River near its mouth at Jacksonville. The late-nineteenth-century writer Abbie M. Brooks, who called herself "Silvia Sunshine," described these "white-winged little crafts . . . constantly flitting about the Jacksonville wharves like summer songsters in a clear sky." Her description of the early morning view of this portion of the river, seen from one of these little yachts, enumerated many of the elements included in Heade's painting: "The St. John's to-day appears overspread with a kind of semi-transparent mist, through which the sun shines with a nimbus of golden sheen, that fills air and sky. Imagination could not paint the River of Life more beautiful. How smoothly we glide on its peaceful bosom, while fleecy clouds of unrivaled purity float over us like airy forms, which leave an undefinable idea of an invisible presence hovering near."[9]

Plate 8: *Florida River Scene: Early Evening after Sunset*, c. 1887–1900

In *Florida River Scene*, Heade uses a high viewpoint to impart sweeping breadth to his composition. The entire panorama is just at the point of disappearing into the darkness that has already swallowed up much of the foreground. The crowns of the palm trees shimmer like aureoles against the last pulse of the afterglow. A pair of egrets poised on a fallen branch are momentarily silhouetted in the dying light, underscoring their fragility and increasingly imperiled status. Heade worried that these graceful, elegant birds would soon disappear entirely from Florida, victims of the plume-hunters who killed them indiscriminately for the sake of a few choice feathers to adorn the hats of fashionable ladies. "In years gone by, Florida was swarming with flamingoes, spoonbills, egrets and other beautiful plumaged birds, but they are nearly all numbered with things that were," wrote Heade. "Now the great question is in regard to the way in which this brutal bird butchery can be stopped."[10]

Even the editors of the fashionable St. Augustine paper, the *Tatler*, raised a prophetic voice for conservation, recognizing that the destruction of the environment and the birds would ultimately endanger Florida tourism by effacing the natural beauty of the state. They proposed legislation that would establish bird sanctuaries and promote the enforcement of existing game laws, and even enlisted Henry Flagler in their cause. Their plea for a scheme reconciling development and preservation reads like a modern proposal for ecotourism: "[We ask] all persons interested in birds and animals and all who are interested in the State to use their influence to secure this legislation. . . . With the restoration of bird and animal life, the value of the property will be enhanced many times, the State will be more productive and more attractive to the tourist and the traveler. With game animals and birds restored, the streams again teeming with fish, their banks alive with ducks and cranes and laws preventing their killing except in the proper time and way, Florida will have restored to her, her natural attractions together with the finest hotel service and transportation lines leading to them."[11]

Plate 9: *Sunset: Tropical Marshes, Florida*, c. 1883–89

This painting stretches Heade's usual 1:2 ratio into an even narrower 1:3 format. This extreme panoramic design emphasizes the expansiveness and horizontality of a sweep of riparian swampland that contains the same basic essentials as *The St. Johns River* (plate 1) and must depict a similar locale. Here, too, we see the qualities of intense stillness and almost mystic communion with nature that art historians have dubbed luminism. Some modern scholars have linked those qualities to the philosophical ideas of transcendentalists Henry Thoreau and Ralph Waldo Emerson, and certainly Heade seems to have been a kindred spirit to those who sought a spiritual communion with nature. Heade's St. Augustine patrons and admirers simply referred to his tranquil images of sunrise and sunset as "restful pictures." The rhythmic variations provided by waterlily pads, clumps of reeds, palm trees, and cattle barely intrude into the softly pulsing bands of color that modulate upward from water through land to sky and cloud. This is one of Heade's most intensely colored sunsets, yet it remains understated. He has waited for the moment when the sun has just disappeared below the horizon, preferring subdued and gradually vanishing effects rather than the more blatant spectacle that might have been visible a few moments before.

By happy coincidence, this painting now hangs in the museum that houses the world's most extensive and important collection of stained glass by Louis Comfort Tiffany. Undoubtedly the two artists must have met when Tiffany was completing the vast array of windows for the dining room of the Hotel Ponce de Leon. The hotel windows are also understated, favoring soft colors and wide expanses of clear glass. This particular sunset by Heade seems to glow from within with something of the intensity of stained glass.

Plate 10: *Orchid and Hummingbird ("Heliodore's Woodstar")*, c. 1890–1904

Heade recounts being fascinated with hummingbirds from boyhood, but he first painted and studied them when he traveled to Brazil in 1864. His intention of publishing an illustrated compendium, to be called *The Gems of Brazil*, was never realized. However, he continued to paint the tiny birds he had seen in Brazil and in later travels to the tropics for the rest of his life. He used the large collection of skins he had acquired for information on coloring and markings and probably relied on his ongoing observation of native North American birds to represent postures and behavior. After 1870 he began to combine images of hummingbirds with another exotic South American species, the orchid. There was a great craze for collecting and growing these opulent flowers at the time, and Heade was able to study and sketch them in greenhouses. His paintings of hummingbirds, orchids, and exotic scenery were pastiches of memory and observation, and he continued to develop inventive variations on this theme until the last years of his life.

This painting, one of many that Heade made during his Florida years, was owned by Henry Flagler. A visitor to Heade's studio in 1892 found him "busy over orchids, . . . having neglected those curious blossoms for some years."[12] The success of the subject with Heade's St. Augustine audience is demonstrated in the report of the following year: "Mr. Heade has disposed of two of his orchids this season, showing the great appreciation of these extremely typical

1. Martin Johnson Heade. *The St. Johns River.* c. 1890s. Oil on canvas. 13 × 26 in. Museum purchase with membership contributions. AP1966.29.1. The Cummer Museum of Art and Gardens, Jacksonville, Florida.

2. Martin Johnson Heade. *Haystacks.* c. 1876–82. Oil on canvas. 28 × 54 in. Courtesy of the Huntington Library, Art Collections, and Botanical Gardens, San Marino, California.

3. Martin Johnson Heade. *Evening, Lake Alto, Florida*. 1883. Oil on canvas. 13 × 26 in.
Sam and Robbie Vickers Florida Collection.

4. Martin Johnson Heade. *The Great Florida Marsh*. 1886. Oil on canvas. 27½ × 53¾ in. Flagler System, Inc., Palm Beach, Florida. Photograph courtesy of the North Carolina Museum of Art.

5. Martin Johnson Heade. *Tropical Sunset: Florida Marsh Scene with Cattle*. c. 1885–90. Oil on canvas. 17¾ × 36 in.
Sam and Robbie Vickers Florida Collection.

6. Martin Johnson Heade. *View from Fern-Tree Walk, Jamaica*. 1887. Oil on canvas. 53 × 90 in.
Manoogian Collection.

7. Martin Johnson Heade. *Florida Sunrise*. c. 1887–1900. Oil on canvas. 28 × 54½ in. White House Collection, Washington, D.C. Courtesy White House Historical Association.

8. Martin Johnson Heade. *Florida River Scene: Early Evening after Sunset.* c. 1887–1900. Oil on canvas. 17 × 36 in.
Thomas Gilcrease Institute of American History and Art, Tulsa, Oklahoma.

9. Martin Johnson Heade. *Sunset: Tropical Marshes, Florida*. c. 1883–89. Oil on canvas. 12¼ × 36¼ in. The Charles Hosmer Morse Museum of American Art, Winter Park, Florida. ©The Charles Hosmer Morse Foundation.

10. Martin Johnson Heade. *Orchid and Hummingbird ("Heliodore's Woodstar")*. c. 1890–1904. Oil on canvas. 15 × 20½ in. Fine Arts Museums of San Francisco.

11. Martin Johnson Heade. *Giant Magnolias on a Blue Velvet Cloth*. c. 1885–95. Oil on canvas. 15⅛ × 24³⁄₁₆ in. National Gallery of Art, Washington, D.C. Gift of the Circle of the National Gallery of Art in Commemoration of its Tenth Anniversary 1996.14.1. Photograph. © 2002 Board of Trustees, National Gallery of Art.

12. Martin Johnson Heade. *Cherokee Roses on a Purple Velvet Cloth*. 1894. Oil on canvas. 10 × 18 in. Private collection.
Courtesy of Berry-Hill Galleries.

13. Martin Johnson Heade. *Lotus Flowers: A Landscape Painting in the Background*. c. 1885–1900. Oil on canvas. 16⅞ × 36 in. North Carolina Museum of Art, Raleigh. Gift of the Sarah Graham Kenan Foundation, in honor of Mrs. Sarah Graham Kenan.

14. Martin Johnson Heade. *On the San Sebastian River, Florida*. c. 1887–88. Oil on canvas. 17¼ × 36 in. Greenville County Museum of Art, Greenville, South Carolina. Museum purchase with funds donated by the Arthur and Holly Magill Foundation.

15. Martin Johnson Heade. *Hummingbird Perched on an Orchid Plant*. 1901. Oil on canvas. 20¼ × 15¼ in. Collection of the Riggs National Corporation of Washington, D.C.

tropical pictures, as the superb flower is shown in its native wilds, the hazy atmosphere and distant hills, all South American in effect; hummingbirds hover near, completing the picture. Mr. Heade years ago established a reputation for such work, adding to it during the past season by the number and beauty of those and similar pictures."[13]

Plate 11: *Giant Magnolias on a Blue Velvet Cloth*, c. 1885–95

Modern audiences have admired Heade's magnolia paintings more than any other works done in his Florida years. These blossoms, despite their robust appearance, are quite fragile and fleeting once gathered. The difficulties encountered in trying to paint such short-lived subjects is evident from Harriet Beecher Stowe's account of her own attempts at magnolia painting:

> The past week we have been engrossed with magnolias. On Monday, our friend D——, armed and equipped with scaling-ladders, ascended the glistening battlements of the great forest palaces fronting his cottage, and bore thence the white princesses, just bursting into bud, and brought them down to us. Forthwith all else was given up: for who would take the portrait of the white lady must hurry; for, like many queens of the earth, there is but a step between perfected beauty and decay,—a moment between beauty and ashes.
>
> We bore them to our chamber, and before morning the whole room was filled with the intoxicating, dreamy fragrance; and lo! While we slept, the pearly hinges had revolved noiselessly, and the bud we left the

evening before had become a great and glorious flower. To descend to particulars, imagine a thick waxen-cupped peony of the largest size, just revealing in its center an orange-colored cone of the size of a walnut. Around it, like a circlet of emeralds, were the new green leaves, contrasting in their vivid freshness with the solid, dark-green brilliancy of the old foliage. The leaves of the magnolia are themselves beauty enough without the flower. We used to gather them in a sort of rapture before we ever saw the blossom; but all we can say of the flower is, that it is worthy of them.

> We sat down before this queen of flowers, and worked assiduously at her portrait. . . . Two days we kept faithful watch and ward at the shrine; but lo! On the morning of the third day our beautiful fairy had changed in the night to an ugly brownie. The petals, so waxen and fair the night before, had become of a mahogany color; and a breeze passing by swept them dishonored to the floor. The history of that magnolia was finished.[14]

Plate 12: *Cherokee Roses on a Purple Velvet Cloth*, 1894

This painting implicitly transports the wild Cherokee rose into the most elegant of Gilded Age parlors. The unruly yet lovely blossoms are presented against a royal ground of purple velvet, showcasing Heade's much-admired virtuosity in painting this fabric. The wild roses were domesticated in the courts and plazas around the Flagler hotels, and celebrated in the pages of the local society paper, which printed this poem and commentary:

The Cherokee Rose

From *Harper's Bazar* [*sic*]

Who does not love the Cherokee Rose?
Wildest, waywardest flower that grows;
Over the earth it clambers and strays,
In runaway chase and rollicking maze.

Tangled and Twisted its course may run,
What cares the Beauty, the care-less one?
Climbing and twining its wind-rocked bower,
Clings and swings the beautiful flower.

Ever bewitching with matchless grace,
A heart of gold, and white, pure face,
It gleams and shines wherever it goes,
In sunlight and moonlight, fair Cherokee rose!

Margaret May

The above fittingly describes the "riotous, clambering Cherokee rose," now a mass of pure white blossom peeping from the dark, green, shiny leaves, the golden heart scarce revealed as it covers and climbs to the top of the third story windows in the court of the Alcazar. A harbinger of the coming summer indeed, adding beauty to the court suggestive of old world palaces, with its splashing fountains and palms, the grey walls rising straight from the perfect arches of the loggias, while here and there vieing with the pure white Cherokee rose is a wisteria, its clusters of graceful bloom drooping and sweetening the air; its neighbor, a mass of orange begonia, while at their feet nasturtiums, brilliant and varied, add beauty; a picture to delight the guest coming from the land of ice and snow, a worthy exterior to the luxury, good cheer and comfort to be found within, where representatives of wealth and culture from all over the land find a charming home.[15]

Plate 13: *Lotus Flowers: A Landscape Painting in the Background*, c. 1885–1900

Perhaps Heade meant these lavish, imported flowers to serve as a metaphor for the pleasures of "lotus-eating" in which the visitors to the Hotel Ponce de Leon could indulge. When Julian Ralph visited St. Augustine in the 1890s, he found the opulence of the hotel and its guests almost overwhelming:

To live in the Ponce de Leon is as if we had been invited to stop at a royal palace. . . . It is said that a famous writer remarked that he had not the ability to describe the Ponce de Leon and its outlook upon the luxurious court and park, and opposing Cordova and Alcazar hotels. I see here no excuse for trying a hand upon it at this late day. It is its general effect, rather than its details, that charms the beholder, and that effect can be described in one sentence—it is a melody or a poem in gray and red and green. The pearl-gray walls of shell-stone lift their cool sides between billows of foliage and masses of bright red tiling. The graceful towers, quaint dormer-windows, airy loggias, and jewel-like settings of stained glass, like the palms and fountains and galleries, all melt, unnoted into the main effect. It is all too fine for some persons, all too dear for others, too artificial for others. . . . I was so perfectly content and thoroughly fascinated in the week I lived there that the place seemed all-sufficient. . . .

To sum up the impression St. Augustine made upon me, it seems that nearly every taste may be gratified there. The quaint old city, with some streets that are too narrow for pavements, and a score of ancient houses that would be notable anywhere else, is in itself a joy. The fishing is good; the sailing on the almost constantly sunlit, ever breezy river is better. The driving and horseback rides are pleasant; there are country walks and orange groves. The old fort is never less than picturesque, and it is prized highly by lovers almost above a certain leafy terrace at West Point. There are tennis and bathing and shopping. Concerts and dances and exhibitions are frequent. All these and more are for the active. For the indolent and the idle there are the loggias and the lobbies of the big hotels, with music every evening, and a grand panorama of life all the time.[16]

Plate 14: *On the San Sebastian River, Florida,* c. 1887–88

Bright Skies and Dark Shadows is the title of a book describing a winter in Florida written by Henry M. Field, a friend of Flagler's who enjoyed his hospitality in Florida when he had been advised to go south for his health. The title would also serve rather nicely to caption this painting, the only one that reveals a glimpse of the Hotel Ponce de Leon, the complex that played such an important part in Heade's artistic career in Florida. Field is unstinting in his praise of Flagler and his enterprises, but he introduces a note of distinctively American pragmatism when he describes the Hotel Ponce de Leon:

Of course this marvelous creation, that has sprung up in Florida, like Tadmor in the wilderness, is the wonder of everybody who comes here, and it is amusing to observe the look of surprise of new comers, and hear their expressions of astonishment. And yet the American feeling will crop out, and after they have exhausted their admiration, one is sure to hear the subdued question, *"Does it pay?"* as if nothing great could ever be done except as a speculation; and there are many mysterious inquiries as to what could have been the motive of this lavish expenditure so far away from the commercial centers of the country. There is no mystery about the matter. A man who has for many years made his annual visits to this portion of the South, till it has become as attractive to him as it was to Ponce de Leon, (when, enraptured by its perpetual bloom, he renamed it Florida, the Land of Flowers) takes it into his mind to create a paradise of beauty somewhat in keeping with the gorgeous tropical vegetation. Fond of great architecture, and having the means to gratify that taste, he conceives the idea of a building unique in its structure and in its surroundings, which shall be a "thing of beauty" and a "joy for ever." Whether it will pay in the common sense, does not enter into his calculations, anymore than it does into the mind of one who gives himself a costly library or gallery of paintings. He does it as an artist paints a picture, for the pleasure of doing it. . . . The best of it all is that his beautiful creation is for the public good. Palaces abroad are for kings and princes. This American palace is open to all—a place of rest and health, as well as of luxury and enjoyment: and he who has placed it within reach of his countrymen, is a public benefactor.[17]

Plate 15: *Hummingbird Perched on an Orchid Plant*, 1901

The orchid in the picture is a *Cattleya labiata* and the hummingbird a Peruvian sheartail (*Thaumastura cora*).[18] Heade continued to paint South American birds and blossoms throughout his Florida years. He always used the same orchid species in the Florida pictures and must have based the flowers on oil sketches similar to the one in figure 42 (p. 73). For the birds he depended on the collection of skins that he had brought back from the tropics many years before, though he must have modeled their postures and behaviors on the local Ruby-throated hummingbirds he loved to observe in Florida. He described his experience with taming hummingbirds in *Forest and Stream:*

> I have no fancy for 'gators, bears, or coons. In fact, I do not care for any pets but birds, and the smaller they are the better they please my fancy.

My special pet is the humming bird and I never weary of feeding and fussing with that lovely little creature. I tame them every year, and my interest in them never flags.

Last spring my wife and I were standing on the piazza and a pair of male ruby-throats—the first arrivals—came hovering round our heads, chasing each other in seeming play, and then lighting side by side on a star jessamine vine within a foot or two of our faces, without the slightest fear of us, which meant, of course, that they knew their ground, and when I brought out the little bottle they always feed from, one of them came directly to it as if he had fed from it all his life. It's delightful to be remembered by the tiny creatures in this way, and nearly every season I have proof of their wonderful memory. This season at least two or three of my old pets have visited me, and all seem as tame as the previous year, but the early birds that are on the migratory move I cannot induce to stay. They nearly all go further north to set up housekeeping.[19]

Text for Color Plates

Notes

Introduction: *Who Will Paint Florida?*

1. Robert G. McIntyre, *Martin Johnson Heade, 1819–1904*, 1. The territory of Florida was officially turned over to President James Monroe's territorial governor, Andrew Jackson, in 1821 after the ratification of the treaty.

2. Theodore E. Stebbins, Jr., "Introduction," in Theodore E. Stebbins, Jr., et al., *Martin Johnson Heade*, 1.

3. Janet L. Comey, "Florida: The Late Work," in Stebbins et al., *Martin Johnson Heade*, 123–26.

4. Theodore E. Stebbins, Jr., *The Life and Work of Martin Johnson Heade: A Critical Analysis and Catalogue Raisonné*, 269–81, henceforth cited as *Life and Work* (2000). Unless otherwise noted, information about Heade's biography and chronology and the attribution and dating of works is based on this text. Stebbins's lifelong scholarship on Heade forms the foundation of all subsequent studies of the artist. A comprehensive and up-to-date bibliography on Heade can be found in this publication, as well as a complete listing of the artist's writings. Stebbins's earlier publications are milestones in Heade studies. Most important are the 1969 University of Maryland exhibition catalog *Martin Johnson Heade*, and the earlier version (1975) of the monograph *The Life and Works of Martin Johnson Heade*, henceforth cited as *Life and Works* (1975).

5. Angela Miller, *The Empire of the Eye: Landscape Representation and American Cultural Politics, 1825–1875*, 238, 240.

6. David C. Miller, *Dark Eden: The Swamp in Nineteenth-Century American Culture*, 68.

7. Joni L. Kinsey, "Moran and the Art of Printmaking," in Nancy Anderson et al., *Thomas Moran*, 308.

8. Edward King, *The Great South*, 384. For changing attitudes toward images of southern swampland and speculations about how these might embody psychological and social changes, see Miller, *Dark Eden*.

9. King, *The Great South*, 378.

10. Julia E. Dodge, "An Island of the Sea," 652.

11. Henry Adams, "Thomas Moran," in Gary R. Libby, ed., *Celebrating*

Florida: Works of Art from the Vickers Collection, 56. Because most of Moran's Florida paintings are sequestered in private collections, the exact count is uncertain. For Moran's career, including his enormously successful western ventures, see Anderson et al., *Thomas Moran*; Thurman Wilkins, *Thomas Moran: Artist of the Mountains;* and Joni L. Kinsey, *Thomas Moran and the Surveying of the American West.*

12. For a comprehensive discussion of Moran's painting, including its complicated provenance, the story of the failed attempt to sell the work to the U.S. government, and the context and iconography of the work, see Robert W. Torchia, *A Florida Legacy: Ponce de León in Florida.*

13. Moran probably meant to show Florida Seminoles, although his natives, who resemble Plains Indians rather than Florida tribesmen, look no more like Seminoles than Timucuans. By Moran's time, the aboriginal Indians actually encountered by Ponce de León had been either wiped out by European contact or assimilated into the Seminole tribes, who were descendents of the Creeks who pushed south into Florida in the eighteenth century. The anachronistic misconception that a Seminole arrow had inflicted Ponce de León's fatal wound was widespread. The error is still commonplace. See, for instance, "Ponce de León, Juan," *Encyclopaedia Britannica Online, http://search.eb.com/bol/topic?eu=62313&sctn=1* 18 February 2002.

14. "*Penn's Treaty*," according to Elliott James Mackle, Jr., "is an idealized version of the European rediscovery of the Garden of Eden and an illustration of the new beginnings Europeans seek to make in America. They come to the new land, they establish peaceful relations with the noble, reasonable savages, they build homes in the garden, and they enjoy the prospect of future harmony and prosperity." See Mackle, "The Eden of the South: Florida's Image in American Travel Literature and Painting, 1865–1900," 148.

15. See, for instance, George M. Barbour, *Florida for Tourists, Invalids, and Settlers*. For a comprehensive treatment of travel literature on Florida in the late nineteenth century, see Mackle, "Eden of the South."

16. Barbara Novak, *Nature and Culture: American Landscape and Painting, 1825–1875*, 39.

17. See Charlotte M. Porter, "Martin Johnson Heade, an Early Voice for Florida Conservation," and Ann Vileisis, *Discovering the Unknown Landscape: A History of America's Wetlands.*

18. See John I. H. Baur, "American Luminism"; Barbara Novak, *American Paintings of the Nineteenth Century: Realism, Idealism, and the American Experience*; and Novak, *Nature and Culture*. The term had its apotheosis in John Wilmerding et al., *American Light: The Luminist Movement, 1850–1875.*

19. Matthew Baigell, *A Concise History of American Painting and Sculpture*, 91.

20. Harriet Beecher Stowe, *Palmetto Leaves*, 71–72.

21. Martin Johnson Heade to Eben Loomis, February 12, 1883, Loomis-Wilder Family Papers, Manuscripts and Archives, Yale University Library, New Haven, Conn. All further references to Heade's correspondence with Loomis are to this repository.

22. Stowe, *Palmetto Leaves*, 235–36.

23. The blasted tree appears in the most famous memorial painting, Asher B. Durand's *Kindred Spirits* (Collection of the New York Public Library, Aston, Lenox, and Tilden Foundation), and in several other tributes by Frederic E. Church, Jasper F. Cropsey, and Sanford R. Gifford. See J. Gray Sweeney, "The Advantages of Genius and Virtue: Thomas Cole's

Influence, 1848–58," in William H. Truettner and Alan Wallach, eds., *Thomas Cole: Landscape into History*, 114–18.

24. Robert H. Fuson, *Juan Ponce de León and the Spanish Discovery of Puerto Rico and Florida*, 114.

25. Wilkins, *Thomas Moran*, 154.

26. Sidney Lanier, *Florida: Its Scenery, Climate, and History*, 88.

27. For a more elaborate explication of the palm tree in nineteenth-century painting, see Katherine Manthorne, "The Quest for a Tropical Paradise: Palm Tree as Fact and Symbol in Latin American Landscape Imagery, 1850–1875," 376–77.

28. Mary Graff, "The Author," in Stowe, *Palmetto Leaves*, xv.

Chapter 1. *Martin Johnson Heade and the National Landscape*

1. Theodore E. Stebbins, Jr., "Picturing Heade: The Painter and His Critics," in Stebbins et al., *Martin Johnson Heade*, 141.

2. Ibid., 144.

3. For the story of the debut of the painting and of its aftermath, see ibid., 144–45. For the truncated biography of Heade in the exhibition catalog, see James Thrall Soby and Dorothy C. Miller, *Romantic Painting in America*, 136.

4. McIntyre, *Martin Johnson Heade*, 2.

5. Stebbins, *Life and Work* (2000), ix.

6. Angela L. Miller, "Heade, Martin Johnson" (updated and revised 27/09/99), *Grove's Dictionary of Art*, http://www.groveart.com/shared/components/…954a284d28ee32&hitnum=1&section=art.037096, March 3, 2002.

7. Theodore E. Stebbins, Jr., quoted by Christine Temin, "The Luminous World of Martin Johnson Heade," M10.

8. Martin Johnson Heade to John Russell Bartlett, November 4, 1858, John Russell Bartlett Papers, John Carter Brown Library, Brown University, Providence, Rhode Island. All further references to the letters of Heade and Bartlett are to this repository.

9. Martin Johnson Heade to Frederic Edwin Church, April 27, 1868, Archives of American Art, Smithsonian Institution, Washington, D.C. (henceforth AAA), reel 5050, frames 981–93.

10. Heade to Bartlett, November 4, 1858.

11. Heade to Bartlett, November 28, 1858.

12. Martin Johnson Heade Papers, AAA, reel D5. Barbara Novak, "Martin Johnson Heade: The Enigmatic Self," in Barbara Novak and Timothy A. Eaton, *Martin Johnson Heade: A Survey: 1840–1900*, 11, notes that since all but one of these are from Church to Heade, reading them is "like listening to one side of a telephone conversation." The bantering tone of Church's letters, and even the bad puns, are reciprocated in the single remaining letter from Heade to Church, a journal-style epistle that was begun on April 27, 1868, but not completed until June 16 (see note 9); for a summary of the letter, see Stephen Polcari, *Archives of American Art Journal* 32, 4 (1992): 37–38.

13. Oswaldo Rodriguez Roque, "The Exaltation of American Landscape Painting," in John K. Howat et al., *American Paradise: The World of the Hudson River School*, 42.

14. Ibid., 94–95.

15. See Elizabeth McKinsey, *Niagara Falls: Icon of the American Sublime*, 90.

16. See, for instance, Adam Badeau, *The Vagabond* (1859), quoted by Roque, "Exaltation of American Landscape Painting," 41–42.

17. Angela Miller, "Everywhere and Nowhere: The Making of the National Landscape," 218.

18. Church to Heade, March 7, 1870, Martin Johnson Heade Papers, AAA, reel D5, frames 644–46.

19. Angela Miller, "Everywhere and Nowhere," 220.

20. Stebbins, *Life and Work* (2000), 50.

21. The most extensive effort to connect the storm paintings to Civil War themes is by Sarah Cash, in *Ominous Hush: The Thunderstorm Paintings of Martin Johnson Heade*, 37–50. Stebbins, *Life and Work* (2000), 27–28, demonstrates serious flaws in Cash's attempts to read these images as cultural metaphors.

22. Stebbins, "Marshes," in Stebbins et al., *Martin Johnson Heade*, 29. For the many versions of the salt marsh, see Stebbins, "Catalogue Raisonné," *Life and Work* (2000).

23. Heade tells how he learned to love nature in his days of boyhood hunting and fishing in "Didymus" [Martin Johnson Heade], "Pennsylvania Days," *Forest and Stream* 38, 1 (January 7, 1892), 4–5. For a list of seventy-six other nineteenth-century "environmentalists" and "nature lovers" whose close sympathy with the natural world began in hunting and fishing experiences, see John F. Reiger, *American Sportsmen and the Origins of Conservation*, 62.

24. "Didymus" [Martin Johnson Heade], "Summer Woodcock Shooting," *Forest and Stream* 14, 7 (March 8, 1880), 132.

25. Wilmot Townsend, "Marsh Shooting."

26. Nancy Frazier, "Mute Gospel: The Salt Marshes of Martin Johnson Heade," 203.

27. The second version is in a private collection; see Stebbins, *Life and Work* (2000), 256, cat. nos. 218, 219.

28. Novak, *Nature and Culture*, 137.

29. Heade to Bartlett, November 28, 1858.

30. John K. Howat, "Heart of the Andes," in Howat et al., *American Paradise*, 247.

31. Heade to Bartlett, December 19, 1857.

32. Heade to Bartlett, January 3, 1858.

33. Heade to Bartlett, September 27, 1864.

34. Heade to Loomis, February 12, 1883.

35. The *Brazil-London Journal* is in the Department of Prints and Drawings, Museum of Fine Arts, Boston (1997.296).

36. *Brazil-London Journal*, October 25, 1863; Heade to Bartlett, July 10, 1864.

37. Katherine Emma Manthorne, *Tropical Renaissance: North American Artists Exploring Latin America, 1839–1879*, 134–35.

38. Ibid., 73–74.

39. *Brazil-London Journal*, January 1, 1864.

40. The most thorough explication of these ideas is in Novak, *Nature and Culture*.

41. Heade to Loomis, December 14, 1883: "We had some of the sunsets you speak of. I noticed it two or three nights. It was probably caused by the burning of an iceberg that was set on fire by lightning."

42. "Didymus" [Martin Johnson Heade], "Taming Hummingbirds," *Forest and Stream* 38, 15 (April 14, 1892), 348.

43. "Didymus" [Martin Johnson Heade], "Hummingbirds," *Forest and Stream* 63, 6 (August 6, 1904), 111.

44. Franklin Kelly, "The Gems of Brazil," in *American Paintings from the Manoogian Collection*, 116.

45. Stebbins, *Life and Work* (2000), 75.

46. "Didymus," "Taming Hummingbirds."

47. Ibid.

48. Kelly, "The Gems of Brazil," 118.

49. Stebbins, *Life and Work* (2000), 75.

50. Kelly, "The Gems of Brazil," 118, first pointed out his observation of the cycle of hummingbird life; Heade's comment about nests is in "Didymus" [Martin Johnson Heade], "Hummingbird Pets," *Forest and Stream* 43, 7 (August 18, 1894), 137.

51. Martin Johnson Heade Papers, AAA, reel D5, frame 739.

52. In a letter to Loomis, Heade says that he was "forced to shoot" a hummer who persistently chased another away from the feeder; Heade to Loomis, September 16, 1884. The comment on husbandly gallantry is from "Didymus" [Martin Johnson Heade], "Hummingbird Pets," *Forest and Stream* 43, 10 (September 8, 1894), 137.

53. Ellen Foshay has argued for Darwin's influence on Heade in "Charles Darwin and the Development of American Flower Imagery." Charlotte M. Porter, "An Early Voice for Florida Conservation," 184–86, espouses a Darwinian interpretation of the hummingbird images. Stebbins discussed the arguments for and against such connections in *Life and Work* (2000), 76–78.

54. Martin Johnson Heade Papers, AAA, roll D5, frame 736.

55. See Stebbins, *Life and Work* (2000), 87–93.

56. Stebbins, *Life and Works* (1975), 142–43; *Life and Work* (2000), 91.

57. Stebbins, *Life and Work* (2000), 307–10, cat. nos. 427–38; 314–15, cat. nos. 455–58; 320–26, cat. nos. 484–509; 349–52, cat. nos. 606–18.

58. Ibid., 103.

Chapter 2. *Searching for the Fountain of Youth: Heade and Flagler in St. Augustine*

1. Thomas Graham, "Henry M. Flagler's Hotel Ponce de Leon," 97.

2. Edward N. Akin, *Flagler: Rockefeller Partner and Florida Baron*, 116. Akin gives the bridegroom's age incorrectly as fifty-five on the occasion of his June 5, 1883, wedding but has apparently made an error in mathematics, since he earlier (correctly) records Flagler's birthday as January 2, 1830. This error has been repeated by a number of other authors.

3. Edwin Lefèvre, "Flagler and Florida," 168.

4. "Didymus" [Martin Johnson Heade], "Notes of Floridian Experience," *Forest and Stream* 20, 17 (May 24, 1883), 324.

5. "Cottage Life in St. Augustine," St. Augustine *Tatler* 7, 10 (March 19, 1898), 2.

6. The renaming of the Shell Road is discussed by Charles Tingeley, "What's in a Name."

7. Heade to Loomis, February 26, March 26, April 13, May 4, 1884.

8. Heade to Loomis, December 2, 1882.

9. Church to Heade, September 8, 1883, Martin Johnson Heade Papers, AAA, reel D5, frame 689.

10. Stebbins, *Life and Works* (1975), 158; *Life and Work* (2000), 142.

11. Heade to Loomis, December 3, 1883.

12. St. Augustine *Tatler* 1, 1 (January 9, 1892), 9.

13. One of the two cottages built by Heade is still standing. The land on which Heade's house and the other cottage stood is now the site of a Catholic church that marks the entrance to the earliest religious shrines of St. Augustine. David Nolan, St. Augustine historian, and Charles Tingeley of the St. Augustine Historical Society supplied this information. For the fate of Heade's house, see chapter 4 in this volume.

14. Heade to Loomis, June 6, 1886; June 22, 1885; December 4, 1887.

15. Sidney Walter Martin, *Henry Flagler: Visionary of the Gilded Age*, 85–91. See also Thomas Graham, *The Awakening of St. Augustine: The Anderson Family and the Oldest City, 1821–1924*.

16. Stebbins, *Life and Work* (2000), 211. A newspaper review comments that, despite the long hiatus in his portrait painting, "his hand has not lost its cunning," and calls the picture "true to life"; "The Studios," St. Augustine *Tatler* 8, 2 (January 21, 1899), 15.

17. See Louise Decatur Castleden, comp. and ed., *The Early Years of the Ponce de Leon: Clippings from an Old Scrap Book of those Days*, 31–35.

18. Thomas Graham, *Flagler's Magnificent Hotel Ponce de Leon*, 7.

19. Charles B. Reynolds, *A Tribute* (St. Augustine, 1910), unpaginated.

20. Graham, "Henry M. Flagler's Hotel Ponce de Leon," 98.

21. Ibid., 101.

22. For complete coverage of all aspects of the hotel and its architecture, see Graham, *Flagler's Magnificent Hotel Ponce de Leon;* Ana Caroline Castillo, "Two Gilded Age Hotels: The History, Restoration and Adaptive Use of the Tampa Bay and Ponce de Leon Hotels in Florida"; and Rafael A. Crespo, "Florida's First Spanish Renaissance Revival."

23. John Carrère and Thomas Hastings, *Florida, the American Riviera, St. Augustine, the Winter Newport*, 8.

24. Graham, "Flagler's Hotel Ponce de Leon," 107.

25. Both the Koppay paintings and the history paintings, by an artist whose name is uncertain, remain in the collection of Flagler College, which now occupies the Ponce de Leon hotel buildings. These works are also mentioned in early accounts of the hotel, including Charles B. Reynolds, *Standard Guide St. Augustine*, 41. The numerous descriptions in the clippings assembled by Castleden, *Early Years of the Ponce de Leon*, mention the Shakespearian ladies (p. 36), but most often refer to the artworks in a very general way, without listing subjects or artists (pp. 8, 14).

26. See Sandra Barghini, *Henry M. Flagler's Paintings Collection: The Taste of a Gilded Age Collector*. In addition to records from Knoedler's, Barghini made use of photographs of Flagler's hotels and homes and a list of paintings that were at the Hotel Ponce de Leon in 1964.

27. Moran penciled a notation in his "Book of Lists" indicating that the painting had been sold to the hotel, although he believed, mistakenly, that it was later destroyed in a fire. The citation from the "Old Book of Lists" is quoted in Robert W. Torchia, *A Florida Legacy: Ponce de León in Florida*, 30n.4. Torchia has unraveled most of the details of the painting's complex provenance (pp. 5–7).

28. Barghini, *Flagler's Paintings*, 55, quotes a letter of December 26, 1901, from Flagler to his St. Augustine housekeeper instructing her to remove the painting before the opening of the hotel and pack it for shipment to Palm Beach.

29. Dr. Terry Farrell of the Stetson University Biology Department assisted me in identifying some of the plants and confirmed my impression that this is an inland swamp rather than a saltwater marsh. For an extensive description of the history and topography of the St. Johns River, see Bill Belleville, *River of Lakes: A Journey on Florida's St. Johns River*.

30. See Gary R. Libby, ed., *Celebrating Florida: Works of Art from the Vickers Collection*, 37, 49, 55, 45. Stebbins, *Life and Work* (2000), 142–45, discusses other artistic precedents for Heade's Florida work.

31. Stebbins, *Life and Work* (2000), 149; Stebbins's additional description of "dense thickets of mangrove and cypress" in the painting is simply inaccurate. Neither mangrove nor cypress is depicted in the painting, and they would not be found in the same environment in any case. Mangroves grow in brackish waters near the coast and cypresses grow in freshwater swamps.

32. Ibid.

33. Doreen Bolger et al., *Art in the White House: A Nation's Pride*, 203.

34. For works sent to dealers and exhibitions in 1884 and 1885, see Stebbins, *Life and Work* (2000), 176; the commission to Loomis is in Heade to Loomis, January 15, 1884.

35. "Ponce de Leon Studios," Jacksonville *Daily News-Herald* (February 26, 1888), 6.

36. For Flagler's projects on the St. Johns, see Martin, *Henry Flagler*, 106–7.

37. Torchia, *A Florida Legacy*, 5.

38. Heade to Loomis, April 11, June 16, 1887.

39. By 1897, one or both pictures had been moved to the adjacent Alcazar, perhaps to take advantage of better lighting. A "tropical picture, in the parlor of the Alcazar" is mentioned in "Artists Receptions," St. Augustine *Tatler* 6, 8 (March 6, 1897), 13; the Jamaica picture is mentioned in the Alcazar parlor in "The Studios," St. Augustine *Tatler* 8, 2 (January 21, 1897), 15. In 1901 the Jamaica picture was sent south to Whitehall along with the Moran (see note 28). Unfortunately, an illustration of *The Great Florida Sunset*, now in a private collection, was not available for publication at this time. There is a color plate in Stebbins, *Life and Work* (2000), 152.

40. "St. Augustine's Great Day," Jacksonville *Florida Times Union* (January 13, 1888), 4.

41. Stowe, *Palmetto Leaves*, 253.

42. Lefèvre, "Flagler and Florida," 170.

43. For all Heade's works documented as having been bought by Flagler, see Barghini, *Flagler's Paintings*, 51–58.

44. Michael Carlebach, "William Henry Jackson and the Florida Landscape," 91.

45. Peter B. Hales, *William Henry Jackson and the Transformation of the American Landscape*, 180.

46. Ibid.

47. Carlebach, "Jackson and the Florida Landscape," 91.

48. Carrère and Hastings, *Florida, the American Riviera*, 31–32.

49. Ibid., 32.

50. *The American Scene* (Bloomington: Indiana University Press, 1968), 459, quoted by Crespo, "Florida's First Spanish Renaissance Revival," 184–85.

51. "Art at the Ponce de Leon," *News-Herald*, undated clipping in Castleden, *Early Years of the Ponce de Leon*, 87. The source of this clipping is not clear, and I have been unable to locate the original. Later in the article a long description is attributed to "a representative of the *News-Herald*." The description that follows is an abbreviated version of material found in a Jacksonville newspaper: "Ponce de Leon Studios," Jacksonville *Daily News-Herald* (February 26, 1888), 6.

52. July 1881, quoted in Frank H. Shapleigh, James Garvin, and Donna-Belle Garvin, *Full of Facts and Sentiment: The Art of Frank H. Shapleigh*, 8.

53. Heade to Loomis, June 16, 1887; for German see Sandra Barghini, *A Society of Painters: Flagler's St. Augustine Art Colony*.

54. Details about the history, fittings, and construction of the studios come from Castillo, "Two Gilded Age Hotels," 72–74, and Crespo, "Florida's First Spanish Renaissance Revival," 234–36.

55. See Annette Blaugrund, *The Tenth Street Studio Building: Artist-Entrepreneurs from the Hudson River School to the American Impressionists*.

56. Sarah Burns, *Inventing the Modern Artist: Art and Culture in Gilded Age America*, 58.

57. "Ponce de Leon Studios," Jacksonville *Daily News-Herald* (February 26, 1888), 6.

58. "A Visit to the Painters," St. Augustine *Tatler* 3, 8 (March 3, 1894), 5.

59. "Art Reception," *St. Augustine News* 4, 5 (February 15, 1891), 12; "The Studios," St. Augustine *Tatler* 1, 5 (February 6, 1892), 12.

60. "Artists' Row," St. Augustine *Tatler* 1, 6 (February 13, 1892), 4.

61. Quoted from the St. Augustine *Tatler* (March 31, 1894), by Barghini, *Society of Painters*, unpaginated.

62. "The Studios," St. Augustine *Tatler* 1, 7 (January 9, 1892), 7.

63. "The Studios," St. Augustine *Tatler* 1, 5 (February 6, 1892), 12.

64. "Notes about Artists and Art," *St. Augustine News* 4, 2 (January 25, 1891), 11.

65. "What St. Augustine Artists are Doing," *St. Augustine News* 4, 1 (January 18, 1891), 13.

66. Ellen Robbins, "Reminiscences of a Flower Painter," 539.

67. For the studio artists, see Barghini, *Society of Painters*, and Frederic A. Sharf, "St. Augustine: City of Artists, 1883–1895." Ellen Robbins actually had her studio in the nearby Barcelona Hotel, but she seems to have been closely connected to the Ponce de Leon studio circle.

68. Sharf, "City of Artists," 223.

69. Heade to Loomis, December 3, 1883.

70. "Chit-Chat," St. Augustine *Tatler* 2, 5 (February 11, 1893), 1. Perhaps the "other exhibitions" mentioned in the newspaper refer to an episode described by Robert G. McIntyre, *Martin Johnson Heade, 1819–1904*, 30. McIntyre, basing his information on a now-lost scrapbook belonging to Heade, recounted that Heade had been offered an entire gallery of his own, presumably in the Fine Arts Building. Although such an exhibit would have provided an unprecedented national platform for Heade, the project apparently fell through when a Philadelphia patron refused to lend an important work. See also Stebbins, *Life and Work* (2000), 194n.49.

Chapter 3. *Mementos from the "Land of Flowers"*

1. *Brazil/London Journal*, November 29, 1863, quoted by Janet L. Comey, "Early Still Lifes," in Stebbins et al., *Martin Johnson Heade*, 57.

2. Heade to Loomis, December 4, 1887.

3. Church to Heade, March 8, 1875, Martin Johnson Heade Papers, AAA, reel D5, frame 673, and May 26, 1870, reel D5, frame 647.

4. Editor's note, "Didymus" [Martin Johnson Heade], "Hummingbirds as Pets," *Forest and Stream* 51, 14 (October 1, 1898), 264.

5. "The Painters," St. Augustine *Tatler* 5, 3 (February 1, 1896), 5.

6. "Ponce de Leon Studios," Jacksonville *Daily News-Herald* (February 26, 1888), 6.

7. "Notes about Artists and Art," *St. Augustine News* 4, 2 (January 25, 1891), 11.

8. St. Augustine *Tatler* (April 1, 1893), quoted by Barghini, *Society of Painters*, unpaginated.

9. "Art Notes," St. Augustine *Tatler* 2, 10 (March 18, 1993), 11.

10. "A Reception at the Ponce de Leon Studios," St. Augustine *Tatler* 3, 12 (March 31, 1894), 10; "A Visit to the Studios," St. Augustine *Tatler* 5, 7 (February 29, 1896), 3.

11. Stebbins, *Life and Work* (2000), 156.

12. "Among the Artists," St. Augustine *Tatler* 2, 1 (January 14, 1893), 9.

13. Maybelle Mann, *Art in Florida, 1564–1945*, 77.

14. See Stebbins, *Life and Work* (2000), 328, cat. nos. 514–16.

15. Ibid., 328, cat. no. 513; 347, cat. no. 601.

16. See Timothy A. Eaton, *Martin Johnson Heade: The Floral and Hummingbird Studies from the St. Augustine Historical Society.*

17. See Stebbins, *Life and Work* (2000), 318–20, cat. nos. 473–81, 483.

18. Ibid., 136.

19. Ibid., 329–32, cat. nos. 520–29, 532; nos. 525 and 527 were in Flagler's collections.

20. "The National Academy Exhibition," *The Art Amateur* 6 (May 1882), 117, quoted by Bruce Weber, *American Beauty: The Rose in American Art, 1800–1920*, 20.

21. "Artist's Reception," *St. Augustine News*, 4, 6 (February 22, 1991), 13.

22. Runnam Ban, "A Visitor's Verdict" (January 28, 1888), in Castleden, *The Early Years of the Ponce de Leon*, 44.

23. "News from St. Augustine," Jacksonville *Daily News-Herald* (January 9, 1888), 2.

24. "An Hour with the Artists," St. Augustine *Tatler* 3, 2 (January 24, 1894), 3; "A Reception at the Ponce de Leon Studios," St. Augustine *Tatler* 3, 12 (March 31, 1894), 10; "The Studios," St. Augustine *Tatler* 1, 5 (February 6, 1892), 12. Stebbins catalogs two of these, *Life and Work* (2000), 334, cat. nos. 539 and 540. Neither of these paintings can be located today.

25. "Plan of the Hotel Ponce de Leon Patio," included in Rafael A. Crespo, "Florida's First Spanish Renaissance Revival," appendix 5. Unfortunately, this plan is undated; Crespo obtained it from an official at Flagler College, but it can no longer be located.

26. Lady Duffus Hardy, chapter from *Down South*, reprinted in Carrère and Hastings, *Florida, the American Riviera*, xii.

27. St. Augustine *Tatler* 1, 8 (February 27, 1892), 5.

28. Heade to Loomis, March 26, November 23, 1884.

29. See Stebbins, *Life and Work* (2000), 336–42, cat. nos. 550–52, 559–77.

30. "Art Reception," *St. Augustine News* 4, 5 (February 15, 1891), 12.

31. "Ponce de Leon Studios," St. Augustine *Tatler* 7, 4 (February 5, 1898), 5.

32. St. Augustine *Tatler* 9, 15 (March 31, 1900), 16.

33. See note 25.

34. Robbins, "Reminiscences of a Flower Painter," 539.

35. See Barghini, *Society of Painters*, unpaginated, and Stebbins, *Life and Work* (2000), 154.

36. Stebbins, *Life and Work* (2000), 161.

37. Novak and Eaton, *Martin Johnson Heade*, 68.

38. Temin, "The Luminous World of Martin Johnson Heade," M1.

39. John I. H. Baur, "Introduction," in M. Knoedler and Company, *Commemorative Exhibition: Paintings by Martin Johnson Heade (1819–1904), Fitz Hugh Lane (1804–1865), from the Private Collection of Maxim Karolik and the M. and M. Karolik Collection of American Paintings from the Museum of Fine Arts Boston*, unpaginated.

40. Roberta Smith, "Nature Caressed by a Hummingbird."

41. Stebbins, *Life and Work* (2000), 159. See also Barbara Novak, "Martin Johnson Heade: The Enigmatic Self," in Novak and Eaton, *Heade: A Survey*, 13.

42. William Bartram, *Travels through North and South Carolina, Georgia, East and West Florida*, 91.

43. John Muir, *A Thousand-Mile Walk to the Gulf*, 90–91.

44. Stowe, *Palmetto Leaves*, 164.

45. See Stebbins, *Life and Work* (2000), 346–47, cat. nos. 596–600.

46. Stebbins, *Life and Works* (1975), 172, identified the landscape subject, although he may not have seen the works in color at that point, because he describes the flowers as "large white flowers" when they are, in fact, pink.

47. "Art Notes," St. Augustine *Tatler* 2, 12 (March 4, 1893), 8; "A Reception at the Ponce de Leon Studios," St. Augustine *Tatler* 3, 12 (March 3, 1894), 10; "Artists Receptions," St. Augustine *Tatler* 6, 8 (March 6, 1897), 13.

48. "Gossip," St. Augustine *Tatler* 10, 2 (January 19, 1901), 6.

49. Margaret May, "The Yellow Jessamine," *St. Augustine News* 4, 7 (March 1, 1891), 1.

Chapter 4. *Poet of Wetlands/Prophet of Conservation*

1. "Ponce de Leon Studios," Jacksonville *Daily News-Herald* (February 26, 1888), 6. Louise Decatur Castleden, "Art at the Ponce de Leon," 89, includes an undated clipping that repeats this description. Stebbins, *Life and Work* (2000), 270, includes this passage in his catalog entry for *On the San Sebastian River, Florida*. He apparently saw it in the original scrapbook that was later compiled and published by Castleden. Stebbins dates the clipping "about 1895" but gives no reason for this dating.

2. In a letter to the *St. Augustine Record* (November 26, 2001), 4, Nolan suggested that the new bridge at this spot should be named after the artist who chose that viewpoint to paint the distant city. I am grateful to David Nolan for taking me to see the precise place from which the artist painted *On the San Sebastian River, Florida*.

3. Martin, *Henry Flagler: Visionary of the Gilded Age*, 102. When he died in 1913, Henry Flagler was interred beside his daughter in a mausoleum adjacent to the church.

4. Martha R. Severens, *Greenville County Museum of Art: The Southern Collection*, 84.

5. Stebbins, *Life and Work* (2000), 44–45, 148; Leo Marx, *The Machine in the Garden: Technology and the Pastoral Ideal in America*.

6. See Akin, *Flagler*, 121; Castillo, "Two Gilded Age Hotels," 62.

7. "The Ancient City—The March of Progress," *Telegraph and Messenger* (Macon, Ga., March 1887), in Castleden, *The Early Years of the Ponce de Leon*, 4. The writer does express his admiration for Flagler's efforts to blend his new constructions into the historical city.

8. Diary of Julia Mary Weeks de Forest (February 2, 1884), St. Augustine Historical Society. This entry was brought to my attention by Charles Tingeley.

9. Heade to Loomis, December 3, 1883.

10. Carol Jentsch, "Martin Johnson Heade," in Ruth K. Beesch et al., *Florida Visionaries*, 17.

11. Nancy Frazier, "Mute Gospel: The Salt Marshes of Martin Johnson Heade," 201.

12. Ibid., 204.

13. Stebbins, *Life and Works* (1975), 22, first clarified the source of the pen name. In the absence of extensive biographical information about the artist, he also went on to speculate that this identification "could lead one to assume that Heade was a doubter, a 'loner'; a sensualist as well as a realist; and perhaps in his own mind, a missionary and—given the strength of his artistic vision despite worldly failure—something of a martyr as well." The characterization is omitted from Stebbins, *Life and Work* (2000) because it no longer fits the fuller biographical picture now available, but it has been overused by those writers inclined to view Heade as an angst-driven loner.

14. "Martin Johnson Heade," *Forest and Stream* 63, 12 (September 17, 1904), 233.

15. Reiger, *American Sportsmen*, 97.

16. Miller, *Dark Eden*, 227.

17. Reiger, *American Sportsmen,* 55.

18. Vileisis, *Discovering the Unknown Landscape,* 149.

19. "Didymus" [Martin Johnson Heade], "Pennsylvania Days," *Forest and Stream* 38, 1 (January 4, 1892), 4–5.

20. Stebbins, *Life and Work* (2000), 147, pairs *Evening, Lake Alto, Florida* with another undated Florida painting, *Florida Marsh with a Tree* that shares the same dimensions. For *Sunset Marshes: Bringing in the Hay,* see Stebbins, *Life and Work* (2000), 269, cat. no. 275.

21. Vileisis, *The Unknown Landscape,* 151.

22. "Didymus" [Martin Johnson Heade], "A Decade Wasted," *Forest and Stream* 21, 1 (August 2, 1883), 8.

23. Editor's note to "Didymus" [Martin Johnson Heade], "Notes of a Florida Experience," *Forest and Stream* 20, 17 (May 24, 1883), 324.

24. *Forest and Stream* 26, 41 (February 11, 1886), quoted by Reiger, *American Sportsmen,* 100.

25. For a complete history of the Audubon movement, see Frank Graham, Jr., *The Audubon Ark: A History of the National Audubon Society.*

26. Heade to Loomis, November 23, 1884.

27. Vileisis, *The Unknown Landscape,* 151.

28. "Didymus" [Martin Johnson Heade], "Birds and Bonnets," *Forest and Stream* 39, 2 (July 14, 1892), 28.

29. "Didymus" [Martin Johnson Heade], "The Plume Bird Traffic," *Forest and Stream* 44, 4 (July 27, 1895), 71.

30. "Didymus" [Martin Johnson Heade], "Buffalo, Wild Pigeons and Plume Birds," *Forest and Stream* 43, 5 (August 4, 1894), 95.

31. "Didymus" [Martin Johnson Heade], "Birds and Bonnets," 28.

32. Stebbins, *Life and Work* (2000), 165.

33. "Didymus" [Martin Johnson Heade], "Exterminatory Peregrina-tions," *Forest and Stream* 52, 23 (June 10, 1899), 445–46. Interestingly, George Shields himself, who edited and published *Recreation* magazine, was credited with the invention of the term *game hog* and used that epithet to caption pictures of hunters and fishermen showing off excessive catches; see James B. Trefethen, *An American Crusade for Wildlife,* 132–33.

34. "Didymus" [Martin Johnson Heade], "Florida Turtle Eggs," *Forest and Stream* 51, 17 (October 22, 1898), 325; "The Florida Manatee," *Forest and Stream* 47, 7 (August 15, 1896), 125.

35. Stebbins, *Life and Work* (2000), 155, 273, cat. no. 290.

36. Church to Heade, Martin Johnson Heade Papers, AAA, reel D5, frame 712.

37. See Stebbins, *Life and Work* (2000), 154.

38. "Artists' Reception," St. Augustine *Tatler* 11, 6 (February 15, 1902), 6.

39. "Ponce de Leon Studios," St. Augustine *Tatler* 12, 7 (February 21, 1903), 10.

40. "An Hour with Didymus," *Forest and Stream* (January 24, 1903), 69.

41. St. Augustine *Tatler* 13, 3 (January 23, 1904), 19.

42. "An Hour with Didymus," 69.

43. "Martin J. Heade," *Forest and Stream* (September 17, 1904), 233.

44. St. Augustine *Tatler* 14, 1 (January 7, 1905), 14–15.

45. Stebbins, *Life and Work* (2000), 177.

46. She disappears from the St. Augustine City Directory in 1912. Before that she had sometimes leased the cottage and stayed instead with friends. See St. Augustine *Tatler* 15, 6 (February 10, 1906), 19, 21.

47. St. Augustine *Tatler* 17, 2 (January 11, 1908), 2. Other accounts of Mrs. Heade in the studio after her husband's death are in St. Augustine *Tatler,* 14, 4 (January 28, 1905), 8; 15, 6 (February 10, 1906), 19–20; 16, 2

(January 12, 1907), 16; 16, 5 (February 2, 1907), 4; 16, 6 (February 9, 1907), 10; 17, 9 (February 29, 1908), 18.

48. St. Augustine *Tatler* 15, 6 (February 10, 1906), 20.

49. See Graham, *Flagler's Magnificent Hotel Ponce de Leon.* When I visited Flagler College in December 2001, Thomas Graham took me to visit Martin Johnson Heade's former studio where we found a stained glass–making class in progress.

50. Dow made a drawing of the plan of the house in May 1954 (collection of the Museum of Arts and Sciences, Daytona Beach, Florida); the house must have been moved during the following summer. By 1955 the address "105 San Marco Avenue" had disappeared from the City Directory. An investigation of photographs of the demolition that took place when the road was widened reveals that the house had disappeared from its new location by the end of 1958.

Text for Color Plates

1. George M. Barbour, *Florida for Tourists, Invalids, and Settlers,* 109, 122, 31.

2. Richard Le Galliene, "Concerning Salt-marshes," 226–27.

3. Didymus, "Notes of Floridian Experience," *Forest and Stream* 20, 17 (May 24, 1883), 324.

4. Heade to Loomis (February 12, 1883).

5. Stowe, *Palmetto Leaves,* 138–40.

6. Edwin Lefèvre, "Flagler and Florida," 186.

7. James H. Stark, *Stark's Jamaica Guide* (Boston: James H. Stark, 1898), 133, quoted by Janet L. Comey, "Tropical Landscapes," in Stebbins et al., *Martin Johnson Heade,* 51.

8. Stebbins rehearses the arguments for and against the unusual identification of the site in *Life and Work* (2000), 272.

9. Abbie M. Brooks ["Silvia Sunshine"], *Petals Plucked from Sunny Climes,* 47–48. Thomas Graham informed me that Brooks was Heade's near neighbor in St. Augustine.

10. "Didymus" [Martin Johnson Heade], "Florida Plume Birds," *Forest and Stream* 48, 16 (April 17, 1897), 304.

11. St. Augustine *Tatler* 12, 4 (January 31, 1903), 2.

12. "The Studios," St. Augustine *Tatler* 1, 5 (February 6, 1892), 12.

13. "Art Notes," St. Augustine *Tatler* 2, 12 (March 1, 1893), 8.

14. Stowe, *Palmetto Leaves,* 161–64.

15. "Gossip," St. Augustine *Tatler* 5, 10 (March 21, 1896), 5.

16. Julian Ralph, *Dixie or Southern Scenes and Sketches,* 173–78.

17. Henry M. Field, *Bright Skies and Dark Shadows,* 49–51.

18. Stebbins, *Life and Work* (2000), cat. no. 608, 349.

19. "Didymus" [Martin Johnson Heade], "Humming Birds as Pets," *Forest and Stream* 51, 14 (October 1, 1898), 264.

Selected Bibliography

Akin, Edward N. *Flagler: Rockefeller Partner and Florida Baron*. Kent, Ohio: Kent State University Press, 1988.

Anderson, Nancy, et al. *Thomas Moran*. Exhibition catalog, National Gallery of Art, Washington, D.C. New Haven, Conn.: Yale University Press, 1997.

Baigell, Matthew. *A Concise History of American Painting and Sculpture*. Rev. ed. Boulder, Colo.: Westview Press, 1996.

Barbour, George M. *Florida for Tourists, Invalids, and Settlers*. 1882. Facsimile, with intro. by Emmett B. Peters, Jr. Gainesville: University of Florida Press, 1964.

Barghini, Sandra. *Henry M. Flagler's Paintings Collection: The Taste of a Gilded Age Collector*. Exhibition catalog. Palm Beach, Fla.: Henry Morrison Flagler Museum, 2002.

———. *A Society of Painters: Flagler's St. Augustine Art Colony*. Exhibition catalog. Palm Beach, Fla.: Henry Morrison Flagler Museum, 1998.

Bartram, William. *Travels through North and South Carolina, Georgia, East and West Florida*. 1791. Ed. with intro. by James Dickey. New York: Penguin Books, 1996.

Baur, John I. H. "American Luminism." *Perspectives USA* 9 (Autumn 1954): 90–98.

———. "Introduction." *Commemorative Exhibition: Paintings by Martin Johnson Heade (1819–1904), Fitz Hugh Lane (1804–1865); from the Private Collection of Maxim Karolik and the M. and M. Karolik Collection of American Paintings from the Museum of Fine Arts, Boston*. Exhibition catalog. New York: M. Knoedler and Co., 1954.

Beesch, Ruth K., et al. *Florida Visionaries: 1870–1930*. Exhibition catalog. Gainesville: University Gallery, University of Florida, 1989.

Belleville, Bill. *A River of Lakes: A Journey on Florida's St. Johns River*. Athens: University of Georgia Press, 2000.

Blaugrund, Annette. *The Tenth Street Studio Building: Artist-Entrepreneurs from the Hudson River School to the American Impressionists*. Southampton, N.Y.: The Parrish Art Museum, 1997.

Boime, Alfred. "New York: A Landscapist for All Seasons and Dr. Jekyll and Martin Heade." *Burlington Magazine* 112 (February 1970): 124–28.

Bolger, Doreen, et al. *Art in the White House: A Nation's Pride*. Washington, D.C.: White House Historical Association, 1992.

Brooks, Abbie M. ["Silvia Sunshine."] *Petals Plucked from Sunny Climes.* 1880. Facsimile, with intro. and index by Richard A. Martin. Gainesville: University of Florida Press, 1976.

Burns, Sarah. *Inventing the Modern Artist: Art and Culture in Gilded Age America.* New Haven, Conn.: Yale University Press, 1996.

Carlebach, Michael. "William Henry Jackson and the Florida Landscape." *Journal of Decorative and Propaganda Arts 1875–1945* 23 (1998): 87–95.

Carrère, John, and Thomas Hastings. *Florida, the American Riviera; St. Augustine, the Winter Newport.* New York: Gilliss Brothers and Turnure, The Art Age Press, 1887.

Cash, Sarah. *Ominous Hush: The Thunderstorm Paintings of Martin Johnson Heade.* Exhibition catalog. Fort Worth, Tex.: Amon Carter Museum, 1994.

Castillo, Ana Caroline. "Two Gilded Age Hotels: The History, Restoration and Adaptive Use of the Tampa Bay and Ponce de Leon Hotels in Florida." Master's thesis, Texas Tech University, 1986.

Castleden, Louise Decatur, comp. and ed. *The Early Years of the Ponce de Leon: Clippings from an Old Scrap Book of those Days.* St. Augustine, Fla., 1958.

Crespo, Rafael A. "Florida's First Spanish Renaissance Revival." Ph.D. diss., Harvard University, 1987.

Dodge, Julia E. "An Island of the Sea." *Scribner's Monthly* 14 (September 1877): 652–61.

Eaton, Timothy A. *Martin Johnson Heade: The Floral and Hummingbird Studies from the St. Augustine Historical Society.* Exhibition catalog. Boca Raton, Fla.: Boca Raton Museum of Art, 1992.

Foshay, Ellen. "Charles Darwin and the Development of American Flower Imagery." *Winterthur Portfolio* (Winter 1980): 299–314.

Frazier, Nancy. "Mute Gospel: The Salt Marshes of Martin Johnson Heade." *Prospects* 23 (1998): 193–207.

Fuson, Robert H. *Juan Ponce de León and the Spanish Discovery of Puerto Rico and Florida.* Blacksburg, Va.: The MacDonald and Woodward Publishing Company, 2000.

Graham, Frank, Jr. *The Audubon Ark: A History of the National Audubon Society.* New York: Alfred A. Knopf, 1990.

Graham, Thomas. *The Awakening of St. Augustine: The Anderson Family and the Oldest City, 1821–1924.* St. Augustine, Fla.: St. Augustine Historical Society, 1978.

———. *Flagler's Grand Hotel Alcazar.* St. Augustine, Fla.: St. Augustine Historical Society, 1989.

———. *Flagler's Magnificent Hotel Ponce de Leon.* Rev. ed. St. Augustine: St. Augustine Historical Society, 1990.

———. "Henry M. Flagler's Hotel Ponce de Leon." *Journal of Decorative and Propaganda Arts 1875–1945* 23 (1998): 97–111.

Hales, Peter B. *William Henry Jackson and the Transformation of the American Landscape.* Philadelphia, Pa.: Temple University Press, 1988.

Howat, John K., et al. *American Paradise: The World of the Hudson River School.* Exhibition catalog. New York: The Metropolitan Museum of Art, 1987.

Kelly, Franklin. *American Paintings from the Manoogian Collection.* Exhibition catalog. Washington, D.C.: National Gallery of Art, 1989.

———. *Frederic Edwin Church and the National Landscape.* Washington, D.C.: Smithsonian Institution Press, 1988.

Keyes, Donald D., et al. *The White Mountains: Place and Perceptions.* Exhibition catalog. Hanover, N.H.: University Press of New England, 1980.

King, Edward. *The Great South.* 1875. Reprint, New York: Arno Press, 1969.

Kinsey, Joni L. *Thomas Moran and the Surveying of the American West*. Washington, D.C.: Smithsonian Institution Press, 1992.

Lanier, Sidney. *Florida: Its Scenery, Climate, and History*. 1875. Facsimile with intro. by Jerrell H. Shofner. Gainesville: University of Florida Press, 1973.

Lefèvre, Edwin. "Flagler and Florida." *Everybody's Magazine* 22 (February 1910): 168–86.

Le Galliene, Richard. "Concerning Salt-marshes." *Harper's Monthly Magazine* (July 1916): 225–35.

Libby, Gary R., ed. *Celebrating Florida: Works of Art from the Vickers Collection*. Gainesville: University Press of Florida, 1995.

Mackle, Elliott James, Jr. "The Eden of the South: Florida's Image in American Travel Literature and Painting, 1865–1900." Ph.D. diss., Emory University, 1977.

Mann, Maybelle. *Art in Florida, 1564–1945*. Sarasota, Fla.: Pineapple Press, 1999.

Manthorne, Katherine. "The Quest for a Tropical Paradise: Palm Tree as Fact and Symbol in Latin American Landscape Imagery, 1850–1875." *Art Journal* 44 (Winter 1984): 374–82.

———. *Tropical Renaissance: North American Artists Exploring Latin America, 1839–1879*. Washington, D.C.: Smithsonian Institution Press, 1989.

Martin, Sidney Walter. *Henry Flagler: Visionary of the Gilded Age*. 1949. Reprint, with intro. by John M. Blades. Lake Buena Vista, Fla.: Tailored Tours Publications, 1998.

Marx, Leo. *The Machine in the Garden: Technology and the Pastoral Ideal in America*. Oxford: Oxford University Press, 1964.

McIntyre, Robert G. *Martin Johnson Heade, 1819–1904*. New York: Pantheon, 1948.

McKinsey, Elizabeth. *Niagara Falls: Icon of the American Sublime*. New York: Cambridge University Press, 1985.

Miller, Angela. *The Empire of the Eye: Landscape Representation and American Cultural Politics, 1825–1875*. Ithaca, N.Y.: Cornell University Press, 1993.

———. "Everywhere and Nowhere: The Making of the National Landscape." *American Literary History* 4 (Summer 1992): 207–29.

Miller, David C. *Dark Eden: The Swamp in Nineteenth-Century American Culture*. Cambridge and New York: Cambridge University Press, 1989.

Muir, John. *A Thousand-Mile Walk to the Gulf*. 1916. Ed. with an intro. by William Frederic Badè, foreword by Peter Jenkins. Boston, Mass.: Houghton Mifflin Company, 1998.

Novak, Barbara. *American Paintings of the Nineteenth Century: Realism, Idealism, and the American Experience*. New York: Prager: 1969.

———. *Nature and Culture: American Landscape and Painting, 1825–1875*. Rev. ed. New York: Oxford University Press, 1995.

Novak, Barbara, and Timothy A. Eaton. *Martin Johnson Heade: A Survey: 1840–1900*. Exhibition catalog. West Palm Beach, Fla.: Eaton Fine Art, 1996.

Porter, Charlotte M. "Martin Johnson Heade, an Early Voice for Florida Conservation." *Proceedings of the 90th Annual Meeting of the Florida Historical Society at St. Augustine* (May 1992): 182–94.

Ralph, Julian. *Dixie or Southern Scenes and Sketches*. New York: Harper and Brothers Publishers, 1896.

Reiger, John F. *American Sportsmen and the Origins of Conservation*. 3d rev. and expanded ed. Corvallis: Oregon State University Press, 2001.

Reynolds, Charles B. *Standard Guide St. Augustine.* St. Augustine, Fla., 1895.

———. *A Tribute.* St. Augustine: 1910.

Robbins, Ellen. "Reminiscences of a Flower Painter." *New England Magazine* (March–August 1896): 440–51, 532–45.

Sears, John. *Sacred Places: American Tourist Attractions in the Nineteenth Century.* New York: Oxford University Press, 1989.

Severens, Martha R. *Greenville County Museum of Art: The Southern Collection.* New York: Hudson Hills Press, 1995.

Shapleigh, Frank H., James Garvin, and Donna-Belle Garvin. *Full of Facts and Sentiment: The Art of Frank H. Shapleigh.* Exhibition catalog. Concord: New Hampshire Historical Society, 1982.

Sharf, Frederic A. "St. Augustine: City of Artists, 1883–1895." *The Magazine Antiques* (August 1966): 220–23.

Smith, Roberta. "Nature Caressed by a Hummingbird." *New York Times* (March 13, 2000), B5.

Soby, James Thrall, and Dorothy C. Miller, *Romantic Painting in America.* Exhibition catalog. New York: The Museum of Modern Art, 1943.

Stebbins, Theodore E., Jr. *The Life and Work of Martin Johnson Heade: A Critical Analysis and Catalogue Raisonné.* New Haven, Conn.: Yale University Press, 2000.

———. *The Life and Works of Martin Johnson Heade.* New Haven, Conn.: Yale University Press, 1975.

———. *Martin Johnson Heade.* Exhibition catalog. College Park: University of Maryland Art Gallery, 1969.

Stebbins, Theodore E., Jr., et al. *Martin Johnson Heade.* Exhibition catalog. Boston, Mass.: Museum of Fine Arts; New Haven, Conn.: Yale University Press, 1999.

Stowe, Harriet Beecher. *Palmetto Leaves.* 1873. Reprint, with intro. by Mary B. Graff and Edith Cowles. Gainesville: University of Florida Press, 1968.

Temin, Christine. "The Luminous World of Martin Johnson Heade." *Boston Globe* (October 17, 1999): M1, M10.

Tingeley, Charles. "What's in a Name." *St. Augustine Historical Society Library Newsletter* (September 1996).

Torchia, Robert W. *A Florida Legacy: Ponce de León in Florida.* Jacksonville, Fla.: The Cummer Museum of Art and Gardens, 1998.

Townsend, Wilmot. "Marsh Shooting." *Forest and Stream* 40, 1 (January 5, 1893): 5.

Trefethen, James B. *An American Crusade for Wildlife.* New York: Winchester Press and Boone and Crockett Club, 1975.

Truettner, William H., and Alan Wallach, eds. *Thomas Cole: Landscape into History.* Exhibition catalog. New Haven, Conn.: Yale University Press, 1994.

Vileisis, Ann. *Discovering the Unknown Landscape: A History of America's Wetlands.* Washington, D.C.: Island Press, 1997.

Weber, Bruce. *American Beauty: The Rose in American Art, 1800–1920.* Exhibition catalog. New York: Berry-Hill Galleries, 1997.

Wilkins, Thurman. *Thomas Moran: Artist of the Mountains.* 1966. 2d ed. rev. and enl. Norman: University of Oklahoma Press, 1998.

Wilmerding, John, et al. *American Light: The Luminist Movement, 1850–1875.* Exhibition catalog. Princeton, N.J.: Princeton University Press, 1989.

Index

All works of art are by Martin Johnson Heade, unless otherwise noted. *Italicized* numerals refer to pages with illustrations.

Roberta Smith Favis is professor of art history and
curator of the Vera Bluemner Kouba Collection at Stetson University,
DeLand, Florida. She has published numerous catalogs and articles on
nineteenth- and twentieth-century American art.